Hopeless

to

Hopeful

Catherine Todd

DEDICATION

To my husband and children who make everyday full of hope
and joy. I love you!

The day was finally here. We were moving Skyler, my nineteen-year-old daughter, into her dorm at a small private school in the Midwest. After six hours in the car, we finally arrived.

Skyler, my bright, beautiful daughter, beamed as she inspected her new dorm room. My husband and I looked at each other as tears welled up in my eyes. Truly, I couldn't believe we were here. Skyler was our firstborn. At age nine, she was diagnosed with a pervasive developmental disorder not otherwise specified (PDD-NOS) on the autism spectrum. On paper, Skyler never should have made it to college. Yet we were here.

We were really here.

As my husband and I raised Skyler, we had the desire, like most parents, to set her on a course for success. For us, this included continuing her education after high school. To be there, in that dorm room, helping her unpack her books, posters, and a boxes of mementos from her bedroom at home, was like a dream come true.

This dream of taking my daughter to college always seemed so far away; at times, the road was so bumpy. Along the way, I often wondered if I would make it. When I say "make it," I mean I wondered if I was doing a "good enough" job. I once heard from a wise woman that most of us as parents do a "good enough" job, and our kids will turn out just fine. I remember hearing this and thinking I wanted to do better than just "good enough." I decided one day, when I was sitting in a special education meeting for my daughter, that being a passive participant in this process was not enough; I decided I needed to do more.

In my quest to do more and understand how to help my daughter, I also questioned my own purpose. I had been a stay-at-home mom for about fifteen years at this point, but really questioned God's plan for my life. As the mother of four children, two of which were diagnosed with special needs, it was easy to feel lost. I found a training program to become a life purpose coach, and decided to fly to Missouri, my home state, and train with an amazing coach named Karen to pursue a certification in life purpose coaching. Karen happened to have background in special education; as we were looking at women that would be my "ideal client," my heart was drawn to women raising children with special needs.

As I started to tap into my "why" for helping moms like myself navigate raising children with special needs, I realized that so much of my journey had been on my own. I felt I was looking for people to help me, and they were hard to find. I decided that in order to be of the best service to moms, I needed to really understand the special education maze. In 2011, I started a three year master's degree program in special education, and I graduated in 2014.

With my diploma and certifications in hand, I realized that I had no more excuses or roadblocks as to why I was not ready to help moms like myself help their children with special needs thrive not just survive. I also knew that God expected me to use my gifts and story to help others. Today, I get to walk alongside moms as their private coach and guide them as they hire me for a six-month period to help them navigate their children's special education journeys, and their own journeys as mothers and as women. What I have realized is that moms underestimate the power their examples set for their children. In my studies to become a teacher, I was taught a great deal about how children model what they see. At this time, a light bulb went off in my head: if moms model an inspired and hopeful life to their children with special needs, won't these same children go on a live their life in the same way?

As I was deciding on the name of my business in 2015, I thought about many of the women I have coached and my own journey, as well, with special needs children; I realized it was like running a marathon. Every day is a choice to stay in a place of feeling inspired and hopeful. We are all yearning to move from hopeless to hopeful everyday. This book is our story, but it is also the story of every mom who has to watch her child struggle to overcome a disability and find a way to thrive.

CHAPTER 1

Idealistic Expectations

I have often thought, if you could begin with the end in mind, how easy life would be. If we had known, when I was pregnant, even, what would happen, "Great! This child is going to go to college!" then we would have known that everything would work out. If we could just begin with the end in mind, all the worries we'd have when we're pregnant, or getting ready to take on raising a child via adoption, all of it would be alleviated. All that stress. That day, taking Skyler to the dorm, moving her in, and seeing that smile on her face meant more than anything. Skyler hugged us goodbye, and with her hug I felt the words exude from her body: "I got it. I got it. I'm ready. I got this."

When I look back to where I was almost nineteen years ago, when I first found out I was pregnant with Skyler, it amazes me to see how far I have come. Despite all that she has been through, this is one child who is doing what she's doing against all odds. On paper, Skyler appeared like one big human obstacle: "She may not go to a regular school. This is wrong with her. That's wrong with her. She may not ever do this. Her IQ is this. She's average. She is showing delays. Blah, blah, blah, blah, blah!" That's what it was—blah, blah, blah, blah, blah. Had I embraced those words on her official diagnosis report as who she really was, I would have just shut down.

Our minds are often protected. We don't see the end. But if I had seen the end, things would have been so different. In some way, for me, it's God. In some way, I was given a glimmer into what her life would be because I never gave up. I never believed how she looked "on paper" would be her reality.

Even from the outset, as a pregnant twenty-six-year-old, I was optimistic. I had been married three years. Once we started trying, I became pregnant right away. Everything worked out great. Everything worked out the way it was supposed to. The pregnancy was easy. I gained a lot of weight. I was really, really, really fat, and it wasn't anybody's fault but my own because I ate a lot of steak. I did everything in routine order. I had my ultrasounds done regularly. It was 1996, so I had the alpha-fetoprotein test done, a common test for the time to measure the alpha-fetoprotein levels in the mother's blood. I had this test done around twelve to sixteen weeks, and they found out that my levels of alpha-fetoprotein were low. I learned that high levels on the test indicate neural tubal defects like spina bifida and low levels are indicative of chromosomal abnormalities. My obstetrician knew that my husband was in his residency and he knew what was going on. He informed us that we could have an amniocentesis done to see if there was a possibility that our child may have Down Syndrome. So I allowed myself to keep my idealistic expectation that everything was going to be fine. Everything was going to be great. There wouldn't be a problem.

We went ahead with the amniocentesis, which was very stressful. They inserted a rather large needle into my stomach. I had heard of women spontaneously miscarrying during an amniocentesis procedure, so I was a little worried. It is a risky thing to undergo. But I did it. Then we waited for two weeks. To me, in my mind, everything was fine.

My idealistic expectation kept me in check, yet still the thought that the risks might apply to me entered my mind. Why do we embark on these things? Why are we willing to take chances like this? Was the craving to know so strong that I couldn't just be patient and discover how my child would be once she was born? I believe it has to do with entitlement. We live in a world where we feel entitled, entitled to know what we want, when we want. If we want to know whether our child will be born healthy or not, then we take the steps to find out. I knew we were entitled to have a healthy child. That was my expectation. "I will have a healthy child. Everything will be great. It's going to be really easy."

At four months, I still felt everything was fine. I was right; God answered our prayer and we found our unborn child did not have Down Syndrome. Everything was good. Heading into my eighth month, however, I was put on bed rest. I quit working because I had a lot of pitting edema and swelling. I was just one big, swollen, miserable woman.

It was fun, I suppose, to be off work, anticipating the birth of my child. The due date of September 25th arrived, and no Skyler. Ten days later, October 5th, I still hadn't given birth. My mother flew in from Arkansas to help me through the delivery and first days. We scheduled an induction. The night before I was to be induced, we went to a movie. I was still so entitled, thinking, "I want to go see a movie. Everything is fine. Nothing is going to be wrong."

The next day, I went in, and they induced me. They had to give me Pitocin, as I was clearly not going into labor on my own. By then, I was ten days late. Skyler just did not want to come. Even though they put me in labor, my body seemed to just…stay. I was dilated about three centimeters, and I stayed like that for a while. Still, Skyler was not coming out. A day and a half of labor, no Skyler. Finally, they decided to stop.

"You know, let's stop," my obstetrician told me. "Go eat a steak."

I was worn out from a whole lot of labor with no result. My husband went to get me a steak. It was so good. I felt entitled again. I felt that everything was going to be good. I ate so much steak during my pregnancy, and there I was, over two hundred pounds, eating steak in the hospital.

The next day, we tried again. Again, they gave me the Pitocin. This time, I delivered Skyler. She weighed 8 pounds, 12 ounces. She was 22 inches long. She swallowed some meconium at one point in the delivery (swallowing her own feces), which could have been one area of risk. Nothing came back on her Apgar score (an indicator of overall infant health) that was abnormal. Everything came back normal. She looked good. She was normal. She was fine. Everything looked good. She was a great baby. I brought her home.

I thought about this again, later, when we found out there was going to be a struggle with Skyler. My journey was different than that of a friend of mine, whose child was born with a syndrome that caused severe physical disabilities. She and I talked about this often, that my child's disabilities ended up being something unseen, so much less obvious than the disabilities of her son.

My story ended up being different than the one my idealistic, twenty-six-year-old self, with a beautiful baby, imagined. It could have been harder, but looking back, I felt guilt that I thought everything should be okay because for some reason I was entitled to it, because I believed I was a good person and I should have a healthy baby. I felt guilty that I thought Larry and I were people who did all the right things, and that we deserved this healthy situation.

I learned not to beat myself up for feeling that way. I think it's part of human nature to feel that way. Now, as a coach, I encourage my clients not to beat themselves up for the expectations they have. Those expectations are often what help get us through times that are challenging. Let's face it; pregnancy, in and of itself, is challenging. We enjoy it, we go through it, we have all these emotions, then we have this baby, and it might even be right at birth where we see that our child has a physical disability. Missing a limb. Blind. Born without an ear. Down Syndrome. Whatever it looks like, for some of us, our idealistic expectations are crushed from day one. For others, like myself, my expectations became transparent when Skyler was between the ages of two and seven. Don't sweat that expectation, and don't feel bad that it was idealistic.

Disabilities and special needs do not discriminate. This can happen to anyone. If we are blessed enough to become parents, whether biologically, through adoption, through fostering, or however it looks, and we happen to have a child that doesn't fall within our expectations, it has to be okay. It is where we were in that particular moment in time. It's okay. I just wish someone had told me that at the time, because the guilt I felt later was really, really tough to deal with. I just kept beating myself up for the expectations that I had.

It was helpful for me to embrace and recognize that those idealistic expectations are part of the process of becoming a mother. However it is that we become mothers, our expectations define and shape the type of mother we are. At the end of the day, I wouldn't do it any differently. I'm glad I was idealistic. I'm glad that I didn't navigate my pregnancy, my journey into becoming a mother, with fear. Had I navigated it with fear, I wouldn't be able to look back and say that I enjoyed my pregnancy with Skyler. There's nothing I would undo. I am so proud that I had her. At the end of the day, she is who she is, and over time, my expectations were met. I don't think I am alone in feeling this way. I know so many mothers who have told me there is nothing they would have done differently when it came to their children. At the end of the day, we're talking about our children. No matter what that child looks like, we're thankful for the gift. For me, this gift has helped me become a better human being. Maybe the gift didn't turn out to match the idealistic vision I thought I was entitled to have, but it was nonetheless a gift. If that idealism got me through my pregnancy or, later, Skyler's diagnosis, it's okay. It is what it is.

CHAPTER 2

Seeing A Different Reality

I was a young mom when I had Skyler, and I think was susceptible to making comparisons to her peers. Well, I think we all make those comparisons. Comparing Skyler to her peers made me notice her differences, and yet I still didn't fully grasp the extent of how different our reality was compared to other families.

We lived in a really unique situation when Skyler was born. My husband, a physician in training, was continuing his education. He was in an orthopedic residency program, which was very rigorous, filled with long hours for him and many nights alone for me. We lived in a dorm situation, where a lot of moms stayed at home while their husbands studied. I was at home, too. Our husbands worked so many hours that us, the wives, would all get together frequently. Skyler had a little buddy who was about her age, a month younger. They played together well. In that first year of Skyler's life, I saw there was nothing really officially "diagnosable" about Skyler. She was talking, somewhat. She was communicative. She wasn't crawling, however. I compared her to another child in the community. This child was younger than Skyler and was crawling. Skyler was nine, ten months old—and I was comparing her to a six-month-old, who was crawling. When Skyler was eleven and even twelve months old, she was still not crawling. No crawling means no walking. It is the kind of thing that sends people to the doctor. She was not crawling and certainly not walking. At seventeen months, Skyler started crawling.

Skyler not crawling until seventeen months was definitely an indicator that our reality was different. I took her to a screening held by a community health group. The practitioner who heard my story told me that if Skyler was not walking, then this could be an indicator of more severe developmental delays. There were other little things that were noticeable, but at the time I didn't know. Now that I am a special education teacher, I understand these things. I have much more awareness around what the red flags to watch out for are. But back then, I just didn't know, and you don't know what you don't know.

I made an appointment for physical therapy to help Skyler with walking. The day before she started physical therapy, she walked. My thinking turned to, "Okay. Skyler just didn't want to walk." I thought the problem was solved. I thought, again, that our reality was okay. Sure, it was a little different than my best friend's daughter who was doing this and that, who was talking and expressive. I thought it was okay that Skyler was not talking that much. Or walking. She was just her own bird.

We carried on as normal. I became pregnant with our second child, our daughter Vivianne. Vivianne was more talkative, pushing her way around life, and protective of her big sister. Vivianne was like a force of nature, barreling through and taking charge. I started to notice things that Skyler wasn't doing compared to her sister. It became more and more clear that the reality was that Skyler was different. I still didn't know what was different, but something was different. I think a lot of parents that I come into contact with, particularly the mothers, have had similar observations. They just knew something was off. Not even necessarily wrong, just different. It seems like a key phrase I often hear when I am meeting mothers of kids with disabilities, whether it's ADHD, dyslexia, a physical disability, Tourette's Syndrome, visual impairment. Whatever it may be, something was off. Something was different. In each case and with each client, mothers defer to the internal mommy sense.

I had another daughter after Vivianne, our third. Katie, like Vivianne, also hit her milestones. I had a fourth child, our son Thomas. By this time, Skyler was five-years-old. I found myself looking at Skyler and then at Thomas, and I would see that there were things that he wasn't doing that were similar to the way Skyler didn't do things. We still didn't know anything officially about why Skyler did things the way she did, and now Thomas too. Once again, there was a different reality. The realities of Skyler and Thomas were different compared to Vivianne and Katie.

The psychologists, pediatricians, and teachers all say, "Don't ever compare your children." But in my opinion, when it comes to noticing development differences, it is almost a necessity. It's an instinct that you have as a mother. This reality is a little skewed. It's a little different. I felt as though I was being nudged. There was an inner stirring. I am linked spiritually to God, so for me it felt like God was talking to me. He was saying, "Hear me, Catherine. Hear me." That's what these little stirrings were. For another person who may not have a relationship with the Lord, it could be someone else who does the nudging. Perhaps their parents or a grandparent saying, "You know, honey, something is not right." After the nudge, the reality starts to look different to you. Whether it's little nudges from other people, or your own inner stirring, these present the reality— which you often do not, or are not ready to, see.

Thomas coming into our lives brought a lot of insight into the different reality we were experiencing. When he was about two, Thomas was displaying echolalia (repetitive speech). For instance, I'd ask him, "What's your name?" He'd respond, "What's my name?" It would be a parrot-like response.

Every time we were generating conversations, there was more repeating. I remember going to church and sending Thomas to Sunday school. It wasn't our home church but a church we were visiting. The Sunday school teacher approached me afterwards and explained to me that she was a special needs teacher. When she asked me whether or not I thought Thomas had special needs, I was shocked. I recall wondering why someone would ever be so rude and inappropriate. To have that woman ask me that, and for her to be a special education teacher was ridiculous. Now that I have an understanding of special education, I know that it is, indeed, shocking a professional would say that to a parent.

I gave her an emphatic, "No!" in response to her question. I was pissed off. Who was this teacher to tell me that my reality is a different reality? This was not her reality to claim. It was mine. I resented her telling me something was wrong with my child. Despite being so pissed off, I was still in church. Although emphatic at first, I followed up the "No!" with, "No. I think he's fine."

At this point I had a six-year-old and a one-year-old who both seemed to present different realities and two kids in between who developed mentally and physically on target. Still, it was nothing concrete, just a different reality. Now that I have studied special education and I've evolved, I find this is a very common story. You're seeing a reality that's different than other people around you. You really don't know what to do about it. You're not at a place where there are any formal things that have been done.

When Skyler started kindergarten, it wasn't long before her teachers began to come up to me. Skyler's kindergarten teacher said, "I've never quite seen a kindergartener like this." Skyler did not want to engage with other children; she would just stand and watch everything happening around her. The year before, when we were in Minnesota for a year while my husband continued his studies, Skyler had been enrolled in preschool. The preschool teacher told me one day that Skyler was "defiant." I thought, "Defiant?" Skyler was perhaps not the most on-target-rule-following, obedient kid in the world, but defiant? I started to believe that was the reality: Skyler's defiant. I remember after bringing her home from preschool that day, I said to her, "You're being defiant. How dare you be defiant."

When Skyler was seven, Thomas was almost two and in preschool. Thomas went to a Montessori preschool, where everybody appeared to advanced and self-motivated. He was licking the wall, and the teachers told me they had never seen a kid act like he had been. Other students were engaged in the various learning centers while he was licking the wall. Furthermore, earlier in the week, the class was playing a game of "Simon Says." Thomas was Simon and proceeded to tell everyone "to touch your penis." That did not go over well in the prim and proper Montessori. I went to a teacher conference, and a teacher handed me rosary beads, saying, "I want you to take these. I've been praying for this child." I didn't know whether to be offended or grateful. I'm a believer in prayer, however, and it worked for me. She didn't offend me on that level. But there was a moment of, "Do you think something is wrong with him?"

I don't think it's any wonder that my client base is primarily made up of mothers. As mothers, we have a link with our children. We are often with our children more. We have nursed our children. We see and hear things sometimes earlier than the fathers do. To me, this is just a universal thing. That's why it was so important for me to let mothers know, whether it's a two-month-old or whether it's a ten-year-old, when you're seeing a reality that's a different reality and you know something is off, don't be afraid to say it. I even said to my pediatrician once, "Do you think that she may have autism? Do you think she could have obsessive-compulsive disorder because she lines up her animals? Do you think she could be…?" I began listing things. My husband is medically trained. My brother is a psychologist. I would hear things. I was asking them, but people who I trusted thought there was nothing to worry about. I saw what was different, and yet everyone I asked was telling me, "No. No. No. No. No." It began to feel as though no one else trusted my intuition. We often hear that a mother's intuition is the best intuition, and I believe that to be true in most cases.

I encourage any mothers I work with to take the reality of those inner stirrings and be willing to look at them. I think had I been willing to look at them sooner, it would have brought my children—and me—more peace. Again, like you'll hear me say throughout this book, you didn't know what you didn't know—and that's alright. You're moving forward.

Skyler was never supposed to do all that she was supposed to do if I had subscribed to the reality of her disabilities. When I dropped her off at college, it was like nothing I could have ever imagined when she was starting to crawl at seventeen months. Honestly, I can tell you today, where she has landed is amazing. Skyler is going to live a purpose-driven, amazing life because she's exactly where she's supposed to be and she's doing exactly 110 percent of things it was thought she could never do. It's the same with Thomas, my son. He is fully engaged, wants to have friends, makes friends, and is getting all

A's and B's at a rigorous college preparatory school. It's totally not what he should be doing based on what he looks like on paper. So when you see that different reality and you get those stirrings, it is my hope you will open your eyes a little sooner than I did. Doing so means maybe you can have a little more intervention than I did and maybe your kids can have things a little easier than mine did. But at the end of the day, I'm okay with it.

My message to you is this: When you feel that stirring, go with it. Everybody else isn't the expert on your child. You are. You don't need a master's degree or a PhD to know your child because you are the one who spends the most time with your child and nurtured that child.

CHAPTER 3

The Diagnosis

G etting the glimpse that things are not the way they should be is what prompted me to start paying attention. It looks different compared to X, Y, and Z. I had peers, siblings, and other family members telling me what they were noticing. The real eye opener came when I discovered that inner stirring was really a calling. Since I've been working with many different women, I have noticed more and more it is a common denominator among mothers. They have that stirring. The mom has that intuition. It just keeps showing up, in different formats. Maybe through a teacher or another parent. For me, that's what instigated the transition. I needed to find out officially what was going on. As it was, we were totally unprepared for the breakdown that occurred as Skyler entered the school system.

Seeing Skyler in preschool and enduring the comments that were made about her behavior and how she didn't respond like the other kids, or do what the other kids did, I just didn't know what to do. She struggled learning to write her name. There was a delay. She experienced anxiety in situations where typical kids weren't. When Thomas came around, the same kind of stirring-to-calling was happening. Thomas was at a preschool, and the teachers told me he was not engaging with other children or making eye contact. If adults or peers tried to interact with him, he wouldn't respond appropriately. I knew something was going on.

I finally took notice when Skyler was in first grade. Even though she left kindergarten, the teacher still told me she had never really seen anything like Skyler. That Skyler was not a typical kindergarten student. Skyler stood on the edge of the classroom not wanting to engage with her peers, almost as if she was a visitor from another world. As Skyler began first grade, it was clear she was behind in her reading abilities. She was pulled into a resource classroom for additional intervention. Still, Skyler struggled.

Although it appeared that Skyler was able to hold her own, it always seemed to me like she was treading water. I saw the same with Thomas. For Thomas, even when he was in preschool, I saw that he, too, was treading water. They were really just in survival mode, both Skyler and Thomas. When Skyler was in first grade, it was like she could just drown at any minute. I was watching it, feeling helpless—as if I was observing her from out of body, watching her from above, wondering what was really happening. I think a lot of us do this. When our kids are in a situation, we flash back to work out what our own lives were like. And I thought, "Well, I remember first grade, but I don't remember it being like this."

I knew that something was up, I just didn't know what. By the end of first grade, Skyler had been treading water all the way up through the end of the academic year. The teacher was was really talented; she had transitioned from a public school where she had seen a lot of different types of learners. She had been previously exposed to children with many different learning issues and disabilities, and she came to Skyler's school with a lot of background knowledge. Knowing this about her, when she pulled me in one day and said simply, "Something isn't right," I listened.

Unlike my hasty response to the Sunday school teacher, this time I was ready to see the different reality that had been presenting all along. This was a turning point, and pivotal to our success in managing the struggle. I had to be willing to acknowledge that we were living a different reality. I had met that one person I was finally willing to hear. I was willing to hear this particular teacher, and she handled me well. She was loving on Skyler; she wasn't criticizing her. She was just opening up the conversation: "Something is going on. I'm not going to tell you your child has this or that. But something's not right, and I don't know what." Her language in conversation with me was professional, and she did not overstep her role. Quite honestly, a teacher is not equipped——nor should one be—with the knowledge to give your child a diagnosis, or even a suggestion. It is extremely unprofessional for a teacher to tell you, "I think your child has this." They're not neuropsychologists. They're not physicians. They're not in the position to tell you what your child has. I emphasize this to every parent with whom I work. It is important to own that and be aware. What this teacher had seen that compelled her to talk with me was that she had asked Skyler to go to the library—which was right down the hall, in a school that she'd been in for almost a year—and Skyler said, "I don't know how to get there." It was like a vertical line, "Walk down this hall. Go down the stairs. Come back." It was a two-step direction situation, and Skyler couldn't get herself there and back. That was the catalyst for me. I thought about how I could tell Katie, Skyler's little sister, to get me things at home, like go upstairs and get my book, and I compared this to Skyler's inability to find a room so close in proximity to her classroom. It really opened my eyes.

Skyler's teacher was someone I respected and someone I was willing to hear. That was vital, especially given we all only hear what we are willing to hear and the willingness may or may not be present. Up to that point, I really had not been willing to hear these things about Skyler. Nothing had seemed so catastrophic in her behavior that it was abnormal. I thought, "Well, she's fine." Talking to this teacher, I realized Skyler was not fine. She should have known where the library was by April at the end of the year.

I put my journalism background to use, and I went digging. I'm a natural digger, a skill that served me well as my stirring became my calling. I made a list of the questions I had that I needed answers to. Top of the list was, "Why can't my child find the library?" But then on the list went, "Why does my child always act like everything is a big crisis? Why does my child stare at me blankly?" All those questions that I needed answers to. I needed to know exactly what was happening here.

It's helpful to make the list of questions. Every list looks different for every parent. Every question on the list will depend on what you are observing with your own child. As I developed my list, I heard about a new and amazing neuropsychologist in town. He had only been in practice a short while, but he had really good training. A parent I knew had taken their child to see him and found the experience positive, but I knew that recommendation wasn't enough. I would encourage anyone to always seek out more opinions than just one, especially just one other parent. Go to your physician. While your best resource may start with another mother, parents have different issues. I have always been the kind of person to have a first opinion, second opinion, third opinion. In the case of the neuropsychologist, I sought out multiple opinions because I knew the evaluation would come with a hefty price tag.

I called my pediatrician and asked if he had heard of this new neuropsychologist. I was a little scared to call the neuropsychologist, I'll admit. He was supposedly great and very well known. Eventually, I summoned the courage and got on the phone with him. He was helpful and kind, and explained his fee structure when I asked. It was going to be expensive. He was clear about the costs, and I made the appointment. Because he was sought after, the appointment didn't take place for a few months after that call. But we had an appointment. When the day came, I took Skyler in for her evaluation.

Taking Skyler in for an evaluation was an experience in acceptance for me. It may not seem like a big deal, but it was a huge deal. I had to embrace the fact that I was taking my child to see someone to determine what was wrong with her. I had to accept something was wrong with her. For many of us, perhaps even some of you reading this, we stay in the reality of: "I'm still looking at that. There's a different reality, but I'm not ready to jump into this diagnosis of what it is." It's easy to stay in this place because the reality is that once you know, once that diagnosis comes down from that person—that qualified person—then you have to accept that you're living in a different reality.

The neuropsychologist did a two-day evaluation on Skyler. I took her at 9 a.m. both days, and each session was three hours long. Skyler was in first grade at the time. I didn't have to wait in the waiting room during the session; I could go out and return at the end of the sessions. I packed snacks for Skyler, and once the session began, I went next door to get a coffee. No sooner was I in the coffee shop when I was called by the doctor's office: "You need to come back. She's anxious." All I could think was, "Oh my gosh! Skyler can't even handle that." It felt overwhelming.

After the evaluation was over, we waited for the report to come back. The neuropsychologist had done a battery of intelligence tests and tests on the working memory, along with several other different tests. We paid the fee, and then we waited. And waited. And waited. This is usually the case when you go to the right people. You're not going to have the answer the next day. In our case, we were actually called in to meet with the neuropsychologist to discuss the results. My husband was able to join me, which was very beneficial. We sat there together as he threw out a couple of things he thought it could be: "She definitely has ADHD. I think she has Asperger's as well." He did not officially diagnose her on the autism spectrum until fourth grade but suspected it in her initial evaluation.

My husband and I both did a double take. "What?"

There's a little something called comorbidity, which we learned about that day. Comorbidity is defined as a disease or condition that exists along with, and often separate from, another medical disorder. So with Asperger's, she may have Attention Deficit Hyperactivity Disorder (ADHD). Along with ADHD, she may have anxiety. Along with anxiety, she may have expressive and receptive language issues. At the time, she was so young. As she continued to have evaluations every three years throughout her school years, these other condition were confirmed.

Knowing what I know now, they all went hand in hand. I've seen parents come in thinking they have a child with dyslexia. Maybe their child does have dyslexia, but their child also, more often than not, has anxiety, which accompanies the primary diagnosis. Comorbidity is common, and it's important to keep this in mind. If you go in expecting to receive a single diagnosis and instead you receive two, or three, or even four, it can be overwhelming.

If you developed your questions going into the evaluation, go back and look at your questions after you have received the results. When you think about the questions you had, that were really seeking to fill the holes in your child's persona, holes that didn't add up, are you going to get one answer for eight questions? No. You will get four or five different solutions to those questions. It is still very overwhelming, but knowing this is part of the process should help mitigate some of the stress of comorbid diagnoses. For us, having Skyler's evaluation meant we could move from my list of questions down to the five problems we needed to address.

CHAPTER 4

Releasing The Shame

We ended up going back to the neuropsychologist with our son Thomas, as well, when he was four. With Thomas, I received both a report and an oral confirmation that he has high-functioning autism. There were other things too. Unlike when we received Skyler's results, when it came time to hear about Thomas, I was alone.

My husband was stuck at the hospital, caught in a situation he couldn't leave, so he couldn't be there. I sat there alone, listening to the results of Thomas's evaluation. Right around the same time, I received confirmation that Skyler was on the autism spectrum. I was hit with all of this information within a 48-hour time period, and I felt alone in dealing with it.

I initially felt shame. I had all this information and a report telling me all the things I could do. I didn't want to own this in that moment. Of course, I came to it later. You know the expression, "Well, jump with your feet first." Let's just jump in. Let's just take it. As parents, when we have a newborn child and they cry and they scream, we're going to do whatever it takes to just fix it. We're going to fix it. Of course, often it's not done in a way that's really smart. Often we're just jumping. Spinning our wheels. It's chaos following us, nothing methodical.

If I have learned one thing, it's this: We have to address the mother. I've had clients come to me in a state of total overwhelm. They're so overwhelmed that they're unproductive. What we have to do is understand that we are not fixing the mother but addressing the mother. I had to figure this all out by myself. I really didn't have anyone to be my guide through it. That's what gave me the inspiration to coach moms in their journeys. It's become my mission and my purpose. It is easy to shut down when we get that information and see all the things that our child has ahead of them. We shut down. The shame is overwhelming. It's not like we're ashamed of the child. There was never a point when I was ashamed of Skyler or Thomas. Never. But I still felt shame, and on several different levels.

I felt shame because it could have been my fault. I thought about my pregnancies and wondered what could have happened that caused two of my four children to have autism. I wasn't supposed to drink a lot of caffeine, but I know I drank diet coke once or twice throughout each pregnancy. I had coffee although I tried not to. I ate a lot of steak, steak from cows that had some kind of hormones and everything that we're being told about now. I wasn't a vegan. It was the late 90's, early 2000, veganism wasn't as trendy then as it is now. I drank regular milk. I drank milk fortified with vitamins. I drank skimmed milk. What could I have done? Another common thing I heard is that sometimes genetics plays a role; a child has dyslexia and so does someone else in the parent's family.

It's common to hear, "Well, my aunt is bipolar, and my child is affected with it." It's really the "shame-blame syndrome." I went through it and didn't have anyone to talk to that could help me understand that it is a normal part of the process. To move forward to help my child, I had to deal with that particular shame at the moment I stepped into my new reality, my new truth. How do I face the new truth of parenting, a truth that is so different than my sister's experience of parenting, or the experience of the perfect little family down the street?

To address the shame, I stepped back and looked at my new reality with a clear lens. I could have asked my physician, the neuropsychologist, anyone whether there was anything I could have done to prevent this. Was it the one or two diet cokes a week that caused this? But just like in a lot of situations, there was nothing I could have done. There was no pre-testing I could have done to find out that my child has autism. If I could have had a pre-screening for autism in the the womb, it would not have changed my decision to have my child. I wanted that child—good, bad or ugly. Whatever was coming down my birth canal, that child was mine. So for me and my belief system, I would never have chosen not to have my child regardless of whether he or she were found to have Down Syndrome, or whatever. I was mothering the child I was blessed with, no matter what.

Most people I've come into contact with that are dealing with situations with their kids wanted their children in their lives no matter what.. There's no shame. Shame or blame is unproductive. I had to release myself from it because the truth is, it really wasn't my fault. It really isn't your fault. Even if you're in a situation where maybe you drank when you were pregnant and something that was caused by that, there is a point where you have to drop the shame or blame for whatever you're doing because carrying it around becomes really unproductive. The truth is that where you're at in any particular moment of time, you have to forgive. It's self-forgiveness and self-awareness.

I was fortunate to have the support of my husband when I was going through all of this. I have worked with clients who don't have that support system—either in broken marriages or on the verge of being totally alone, with only a grandparent to help them. You just have to ask, "Is the shame productive, and is the shame that I'm feeling going to do anything that's beneficial for my child or myself?" I remember crying and bantering back and forth with my husband. We're not in a perfect marriage, but we have each other. Through thick and thin, we have each other. I remember him saying once, "Well, that's your genes." And I would say, "No. Your long-lost second or third cousin has this." We did a lot of that, back and forth. We were shaming each other, and it wasn't helpful. I was raised by an amazing mother who told me at the time, "Always look at you. Go back to you." I would reach out to her, "Can you believe this is happening?" She would say, "Go back to you and what you know to be true. Catherine, is there anything that you've done in the world that you should feel ashamed that this is happening to you or your kids? Is this your fault?" And I would say, "No."

Engaging in dialogue with someone who gets you, like a rock solid best friend, is a powerful support when dealing with shame. You have someone, even if sometimes you have to go outside your friends circle. My clients often use me as that someone, a coach to walk them through their emotions because I have experienced this journey. Even if you think you cannot afford it, it is an investment in yourself. We're often so willing to hire tutors for our children or pay for special programs, yet we don't do it for ourselves.

The truth is that there's nothing any of us could have done differently, and even if there were, we have to cultivate the self-love to say, "Shame is unproductive. That is unproductive shame, and nothing is going to be beneficial to my child if I carry that shame." We have to let it go; it's that easy. Just simply let it go.

CHAPTER 5

Never Walk Alone

As I released the feelings of shame, I started to take inventory of the people I had around me in my life. Even though I had let go of that shame, there was a feeling of isolation, somewhat like I was on an island. I felt like I was in the movie *Castaway* with Tom Hanks. I was lost on the island. I didn't even have my own "Wilson" (the little volleyball friend Tom Hanks had in that movie). I eventually evolved to a place where I could process all of my shame and know my truth and talk myself out of it. A lot of this has to do with the support I have, which I sought out. I wasn't always like that. Before I actively sought support, I definitely had that feeling of being like Tom Hanks on that island. A deep amount of sadness in me developed when I realized that people that I thought would understand or I presumed should understand just didn't. My husband, my sister, people that were my go-to people in my life, just didn't seem to understand or give me the support I needed. This was new for everybody, yet I had an expectation that people really got it, but they didn't. They didn't. It also was not their responsibility to handle this for me.

It was a journey. This is a recurrent theme that is pervasive in my client population of moms who seek me out. For some of these people, their journey of isolation has lasted years. It can be years for some people because they just don't know what is happening with their child. It took a long time before we knew anything conclusively with Skyler. By the time

I officially knew, Skyler was almost nine-years-old. So that's nine years of isolation, nine years of comparisons. I felt like I was a leper, like in biblical times, a leper that nobody wanted to touch. Of course, it was really me that was creating this, an internal leprosy. My inability to embrace the people around me because I kept feeling like they just didn't get it is really what isolated me.

I've been working in the community of individuals affected with disabilities and living this myself with my children, so I know that it is a very isolating thing. You have to find the ability within yourself to reach out. It's a really hard thing to do. I think personally what I saw was that I would go inward in the early days. I would have something that happened to me that greatly affected me or Skyler—maybe she would hurt by another child, and I would process this pain for her and would develop almost like a post-traumatic stress that would come up way after the event occurred.

At Skyler's school, from kindergarten to fifth grade, they held mother-daughter campouts. I had a turn organizing these for several years, and although it gave me control over the situation, I didn't feel better about it. The tradition with these campouts had been that when the kids arrived, they would first run and claim their bunks. Everybody would claim their bunk and, of course, who they would sleep near. Usually if their daughters were paired up, the moms would also pair up.

Year after year, however, I would go with Skyler on these campouts, and I would watch her little face, and I knew that the other girls weren't choosing to sleep by her. I knew I wasn't crazy. I was seeing that, and I also took it personally. The girls didn't want to sleep by Skyler; the moms didn't want to be around me, or so I thought. I had the expectation that the moms would understand, and they didn't. Nobody understood what I was going through. Meanwhile, Skyler loved going on these campouts. She loved animals. She's so sweet and loved the little animals, and that's why she went. Skyler could run behind the group of girls, not really included, but she would run behind them and find some type of joy. Although several moms did end up becoming my friends, I kept believing they were never going to "get it." They would talk about invitations their daughters received to social events, and I would feel angry at times. Sometimes I would wonder if they were telling me these things to hurt me. I couldn't believe they didn't have a clue or couldn't see my situation. I wanted them to feel empathy, yet I felt surrounded by people who did not understand me. At the time, anger was my predominant response to this.

You can't really walk with people, though, when you're mad at them. I see a lot of that. There are a lot of angry people. You have to let yourself feel that anger. Sure, it really wasn't always supposed to turn out like this for me, and it really wasn't supposed to turn out like this for Skyler, and later Thomas. By then, we gave up on the campouts. My husband was in charge. Thomas started hunting with my husband, and they created their own bonding event. He did not put himself through the father/son campout at school.

My husband's response to both Skyler and Thomas revealed to me that men process things differently. There I was, feeling loneliness and as if nobody understood, and when I watched my husband deal with Thomas, I saw a really beautiful spirit. I never saw him turn inward and blame himself. Sometimes I misinterpreted it as his being insensitive. "You're just insensitive," I would say to him. "You don't see my struggle. I'm watching my daughter feel alone, and then I'm alone because I feel like the mothers and the daughters are rejecting me." But in reality, it was I who was doing the rejecting. It took being honest about this and also embracing the fact that there are very few people in the world who will ever truly understand me, as well as understanding that I couldn't keep expecting random people to understand me—or become angry when they didn't. When I looked at my husband's mechanism of protecting himself, I saw a level of detachment that I did not have.

My husband and I processed it differently. The biggest mistake I made was taking it personally. I would see a little girl rejecting my daughter and take it to heart. Sitting by the campfire and watching the mom allow her daughter to reject mine, to allow her little girl to not include mine, it was hard not to feel hurt and angry. It was my own overwhelming isolation on that little island of autism, ADHD, language processing, anxiety…my little island, overwhelmed with all the issues my child had and sitting next to mothers who just couldn't identify with that. I kept myself isolated, too, because I was unwilling to let anyone in. I just was in so much pain. The way I finally got myself to get my life raft and get off the island and say, "Hey, I'm here. Come pick me up in your little vessel!" was to realize it's hard to engage in a friendship with a broken person—and I was broken. I had to be able to say, "Sometimes I feel really broken, and I hate going to these campouts."

I am blessed to have a dear best friend in my life right now, someone I see on a daily basis. It's my friend, Lisa. Lisa has four children and a full time job, but this doesn't stop her from being an immaculate housekeeper, fantastic cook, and committed in her love for Jesus. She has really always invested in me. From the outside, I'd look at Lisa's kids and think, "They don't have any problems." Instead of writing her off, thinking she would never understand me, I chose to let her in. Her stress was different than mine, but instead of judging her and thinking she'd never get it, I chose to give her a window into our life, into our souls, into our daily existence with all these different disabilities we were facing. I would often laugh and say, "Oh, the Todd household is just a household of issues with all our kids, not just the two that might have official diagnoses." When I started having a sense of humor about it and allowed select people in my life, I found myself breaking out of the isolation I was experiencing. Most people that know me know that I'm an open book now.

I started to know with whom I could be authentic. To share our authentic self is to stop being alone. Those first steps in the early days, where I had to find people that understood and really were my life vessels, were difficult but vital. My friend Lisa and I are like-minded. Lisa and I had our own struggles. Investing with her made my situation not seem so isolating. We walked together with different issues, and we shared our faith experience. We're both Christians, and at times our friendship has felt like that famous *Footprints* story, where there was only one set of footprints because that other person was carrying you. In reality it is Jesus carrying us, but I often have felt, as Lisa and I have our daily phone calls, Jesus put her here to carry me.

Lisa became that one person. It wasn't my husband because he processed things so differently. Some women may have a different experience, but I know many of the women with whom I work are married to men who process things entirely differently. I did not expect my husband to get me off that island. Some people would say, "Well, that doesn't sound like a healthy relationship." It's what worked for me. It only made me more distraught that I couldn't totally open up to him because he didn't totally get me. I'm an emotional, relational kind of person. He's an action-oriented doer. If I was depressed, he'd say, "Solve the problem." Having Lisa as my lifeboat was helpful and necessary.

CHAPTER 6

Nurture Your Relationships

Now that I'm in my mid-forties, I find as I look back upon the people throughout my life, whether it be high school, college, graduate school, or beyond, that my friends, young moms, older moms, and mentors, were always certain people I could have an authentic, intimate connection with. My lifeboat friend, Lisa, is definitely an example of this. I invested in her, and she invested in me. It's mutual. We want to be involved in each other's lives we have made a choice to be. There are other people that I've been just as connected with throughout my life that are just as valid, even if I don't talk to them every day—it might be more like once every six months. Although I invest in Lisa heavily, however, I know it's necessary to keep nurturing all my other relationships. It's important to keep relationships in balance. What it really comes back to is why I was withholding that ability to nurture. There were things within me that were broken. I had a fear of really investing in other people, including my husband and, maybe on some level, my kids, both the ones that were struggling and the two that didn't have disabilities. It became a fear of nurturing these relationships because I was dealing with so much brokenness within my own soul.

I had to step back and take inventory of everyone in my life and really see where I was holding my weight in those relationships, as a mother, as a wife, as a daughter-in-law, as a daughter. I feel I have a responsibility to others. I was raised by parents who taught me and my four siblings this motto: To whom much is given, much is required. As an adult, I found that even though I was dealing with the disabilities of my children and the diagnoses of their disabilities, I still felt like a lot was required of me. I have never let that expectation of myself go, the expectation that I have a big life to live. I want to leave a legacy that my God, my spouse, kids, and others who know me will be proud of. That I didn't just sit back because I could. I got off the porch and I ran with the big dogs.

When I looked at all my relationships, I asked myself, "Am I giving enough?" Let's start with a very important person for me, my husband. Often I will ask myself, "Am I giving enough to Larry? Am I taking the time?" I invest so much in my easy relationship. I notice it when I talk with other moms or peers who say, "You know, I'm not doing well with my husband." I'm not a counselor, but in my coaching business I do encounter mothers who share with me things that are going on between them and their husbands, and from there, we start digging deep within. Doing this work myself, I had to look at myself and look back to those young days of our early marriage as well as to 15 years into our marriage. I thought to myself, "I'm investing a lot, and I'm keeping busy with talking to this friend or doing this or that activity. What am I investing in Larry? How am I nurturing Larry in the commitment I made to him in our marriage?"

What I started to realize, and I've since come to see this as a common occurrence, is that when we struggle with the despair we have for our children, specifically our child's disability, it is easy to engage in superficial fighting with those around us. It was not anything I blamed on the kids, but it created an underlying, overwhelming pressure and heaviness on our family that we all dealt with. I had to open my eyes to the way we were all processing this pressure—Larry, me, all the kids.

I would look to Larry and expect him to be my savior as my husband. The way I saw it, it was his job. I married him so he'd be there to listen to me, solve problems for me. I needed him to solve how I was going to get the kids to this therapy or that program. I needed him to help me deal with the emotion of watching my children be excluded from social events. I remember volunteering to stuff mailboxes for Skyler in elementary school. Basically that involved me sorting all the students papers and communication that went home in their weekly folder. I would see birthday party invitation students would hand out and become aware she was not being included. I would come home with these huge emotions and want to talk to Larry about it, but he was internally processing his own emotions. Our way of nurturing each other often became about taking it off the table, and not talking about it. Doing this somehow let the pressure not define our marriage or our interpersonal connections and the way we validated each other.

I started making conscious decisions in my life and relationships, and since then it's become part of what I guide clients to do. We have to make the conscious decision to say, "My life does not have to become my child's disability. I have to open my eyes to my spouse and see where they're at, too." We were just simply being alive some evenings, when we'd come home and have five minutes to sit down. In that time, Larry would turn the TV on to relax. When we were younger, if I tried to talk to him, he turned it up louder. Now he actually puts it on mute and listens to me because we've evolved in our relationship. I hope it's because he knows that I care about what's going on with him that is unrelated to him being a father. For my part, I've grown to see him as a human being and nurture our relationship, knowing he is not responsible for saving me. I'm responsible for my emotions. There was an expectation when we made a commitment and got married that he'd be there for me, and he has been. He doesn't always do well, and I don't always do well, but we're showing up for each other, and not with an expectation of, "What are you going to do for me?" I think it's a work in progress; we're learning how to show up for each other without being so consumed by our own journeys.

I try to pay attention to my other two children, sandwiched in the middle of Skyler and Thomas, and how they process it all, too. Sometimes I think there was more I could have done for them, and there's more I still could do, but I suppose there always will be. But I had to look at them as individuals in this family. I watch Katie with Thomas and see how she has always been so sweet and nurturing to him. She is the third child, he's the fourth, and she has this creative and amazing spirit and ability to just be there for him. Thomas would tell me, "I love her. I love her. She loves me." They shared a bedroom when they were little, and they developed a nurturing connection that came so naturally. He loves her so much that he informed her he uses her toothbrush when he can't find his own. Needless to say that does not go over well, but her reaction was mild compared to what his other sisters would have done.

For me, it was natural to gravitate towards my oldest and youngest children, my children that were wounded. They had a wound I had to heal. For the middle two children, I didn't see their wounds. Vivianne, my second oldest, was so confident and able to deal with things herself, and maybe I expected her to be kind of like me and tell me what was going on with her. I remember her trying to unload and tell me what was going on very rarely when she was little; overall she was a daughter who didn't tell me her problems. So it was a big deal that she was trying to say, "Hey, listen. Are you hearing me? Are you hearing me?" I remember my response was along the lines of, "Well, yes, I get that it's hard for you, but you don't have autism and you don't have anxiety and you get invited to people's houses all the time, and your brother is not going anywhere." She was trying to connect with me, trying to nurture her relationship with me, trying to invest in me, and I was stuck on comparing, letting her know she could have had it so much worse.

As parents, we run the risk of making that mistake. Was it valid for me to get stuck on comparing and ignoring her needs? No. I had to find a way to show up for her and say, "You know, I know. That's not fair." Thankfully, I eventually got it. I went back to Vivianne, and I told her I knew it wasn't fair for me to say. I recognized I was always telling her that life could be so much harder and it wasn't fair. I was ready to let her know I heard her and I was sorry. I was willing to humble myself to her in order to nurture that relationship. She is now getting ready to leave for college in the fall, and even though she may not admit it, I think she likes to tell me her problems.

My husband and I have a running joke from early in our marriage where I'll say, "You never say you're sorry," and he'll reply, "It's because I'm very rarely wrong." Sometimes I'll retort, "Do you really think you're not wrong?" to which he'll reply, "I'm really not." Then I look at him and laugh. I think about that because it's hard to own when we're wrong sometimes. I was wrong in my response to Vivianne. I had to stop telling her to just be there for Skyler or Thomas because their lives were so much harder than hers. I had to tell her I was wrong, and that is when I began to really hear her and be there for her. It took me dealing with my own inner stuff and allowing myself to be vulnerable around her for our relationship to grow.

Nurturing your relationships includes making yourself vulnerable to your family, even to the teenagers, the ones you're supposed to be strong for. Yet showing your vulnerability and being real not only strengthens your relationship, it also models to your teenagers the power in being vulnerable. Being able to be real brings light into your other relationships and allows you to grow closer. I am currently living in teenage melodrama a lot these days, and I find I make many mistakes, but I am always trying.

I also sometimes forgot that my children were individuals. Another example with Vivianne was that I would overlook her strength. She is so strong. She knew her value, even in early high school. I recall asking her about a boy she liked and her replying, "Yeah, I liked him, but no boy is worth my self-esteem." When I was a high school girl, if a boy so much as looked at me the wrong way, I was crushed. I was always, and still am, highly sensitive. Vivianne is not. So I'd often consider her as though she was the same as me. As she's gotten older, I've noticed the confidence she has, and I've told her how much I admire her. I think back to who she was as this little girl that was so confident on the playground. One time in particular, when Skyler was four and Vivianne was two, Skyler was riding on a little horse ride she loved when a little boy came up and said, "It's my turn!" and shoved Skyler off. Skyler was so sad. Vivianne watched that boy, and it was clear she was not going to let the injustice of this situation happen to Skyler. She went over to the boy and said, "You need to give my sister a turn," in her little vocabulary that was way beyond her years. I think, looking back, that I saw a little girl with a spirit so strong that I forgot I needed to nurture her too.

It's common for some families to have that one kid that we think doesn't need us. Vivianne probably got the least of me because I didn't think she needed it, and my way of connecting with her was to take her out shopping or to do something else she liked as I tried to learn her love language.

I can see how I have let relationships slide throughout my life. The relationships started to slide because the children that needed more from me consumed me. Many people have relationships that end up unsuccessful or in states that are hard to repair because they have focused too much on the struggles of their children with special needs. You don't want to get to the broken place where things become irreparable. Strong relationships are the most effective support for any parent who is raising children with disabilities Nurturing the relationships that make up your core network will make you stronger. As we discover in later chapters about building the team and the tribe around you and child, you'll understand why nurturing these relationships are so important.

CHAPTER 7

Reframing Your Outlook

A fter I began building these relationships around me and filling them up and making sure that I was in a healthy place, there were still peaks and valleys all the way. It's important to remember that as you navigate your child's disability from the date that you find out—or even before—there will be peaks and valleys and we have to learn to ride the waves. What we learn to do is have perspective. Someone asked me once, "Look at the situation. Is this going to matter in nine minutes? Is this going to matter in nine days? Nine months? Nine years?" When we experience different stressors and ask ourselves these internal questions, we start to truly realize what is important. If I don't have that internal gauge of knowing what is important, then I won't be able to create an outlook that has endurance for this marathon. Even though at times it feels like it's a sprint, it's a marathon.

Creating analogies has been both cathartic and therapeutic. I've run a couple of marathons, and I didn't do them because I love running. A lot of things that I have done in life I've done not because I enjoyed doing them but because they were necessary to help me through the times when things were tough. Marathons have become popular, likely because so many people want to test their endurance. Navigating the journey of your child's disability is not that much different; you need to create a mindset of endurance. For me, running marathons helped cement my outlook into one that would consistently provide the endurance I needed. Jeremiah 29:11

> "For I know the **plans** I have for you," declares the Lord, "**plans to prosper** you and not to harm you, **plans** to give you hope and a future." (Source - https://www.BibleGateway.com/)

Consistency is the key. You have to be able to take baby steps consistently to get to your goals, both the smaller, daily goals and your ultimate goal. For us, our ultimate goal was to get Skyler off to college. To give her a running start at post-secondary education. We had to take an honest look: were we really equipped to do this? Of course, we were, in large part thanks to the work I had done setting my mindset. After all, how can you lead someone else to the level of expectation and greatness that you're hoping for when your own mindset is damaged? Creating consistency within yourself and how you approach things will enable you to help your child create a consistency in how they take steps in their own life. Often when I come into contact with moms who want to work with me, I see we are starting from a place where they are inconsistent and in a downward spiral.

If I'm truthful, I know where these moms are coming from because, of course, it's happened to me. It has happened and it does happen, but because I have trained myself and I have aligned myself with people, professionals included, I can get back on the endurance track much faster. I've actually hired coaches myself for many different things throughout this journey. Now when people reach out to me and they say, "Catherine, look at Skyler. Look at Thomas, what he's been able to do. Like from here to here, he's amazing. How did you get that? What did you do?" They know that I have been through it, and they can see the payoff of my hard work. It's like when you know someone has been on a diet and you see the evidence of weight loss, you want to know how they did it. When we find something that works, we want to copy it so we can make that success transition into our own lives.

There is so much truth to the fact that your mindset and outlook are what help the most in creating a path of success for your children. How do you find that path? I took that outlook of despair in the process I went through—the shame, the walking alone, the trying to nurture my relationships—and I stepped away from all of that, looked at myself, and said, "How can I create a mindset and an outlook that's going to have a long-lasting impact on the direction of the life my child has?" I broke it down into a three-step process: first, asking, "Who am I?" then, "Who is that I want my child to be?" and finally, asking, "How can I expect my child to be that when I'm not modeling what they need to see?" This three-step process of asking these questions turns the process inward as these questions inevitably bring us to realize that finger is really pointing at ourselves. We cannot have expectations of our child that we're not delivering ourselves, and how we view things starts with how we look at them.

A dear friend of mine from college shared with me once that the environment we are in shapes our beliefs. If I believe I am nothing, do I become nothing? I think that is so true. It's nurture versus nature. I personally know that depending upon how I look at a situation, what I believe to be true is often what ends up happening. I knew that if I didn't portray and shine with this light of hope and courage to my children, how would they ever do what I expected them to do?

When I was a student teacher, this amazing teacher that I worked with said to me, "If you're going to set high expectations, you'd better get high support." She was saying that, in the context of educating a child and as a special education teacher, when you're going to expect something, you better offer the supports and the accommodations on that child's education plan to meet that expectation. If you're not providing that support, that child is not going to thrive. As a teacher, that is my job.

To tie this back into the situation with my own kids, if I didn't have high expectations for myself, how could I give them the support that they needed to get to the expectations I was setting for them? It was like a vicious circle. I happened to be raised by parents who surrounded us with Dale Carnegie and with Zig Ziglar and all of the success-through-positive-mental-attitude rhetoric. When I was fourteen, my mom said to me frequently, "PMA all the way." (That was "positive mental attitude.") Ultimately, your view of what's happening is based on the lens of how you see things.

Let's face it. For a lot of the time when our children are with us, more than anything, your lens becomes their lens. What do you want their lens to be?

CHAPTER 8

So This Is My Child

When you have a child with a disability, every three years they are evaluated, normally in the public school system(referred to as ETR-evaluation team report.) These evaluations give you a snapshot of how your child is doing.

These reports can be up to ten pages long or more and are basically a biography of your child. It was not unlike the same paperwork we were handed at the time of diagnosis. Recall we received a big chunk of paperwork when Skyler (and later Thomas) were diagnosed. These evaluation reports are the same. In our case, we hired someone independently to handle the evaluation because my children attended a private school. The person we hired completed the evaluation and gave us a report that was a snapshot of Skyler's diagnosis.

Before I finished my master's degree, I would get these ten-plus-page reports for Skyler and have a hard time wading through them. Now, I have people that come to see me, asking me to tell them what things mean in these evaluations. I recall an early evaluation of Skyler's; I didn't even understand what it was saying. I knew that this was Skyler in black and white, but I didn't really understand. I remember reading words like "severe cognitive rigidity," descriptions of Skyler as, "anxious, underperforms at social and academic endeavors." To me, had I not adjusted my outlook to be positive, it would have been all too easy to interpret the entire thing as very negative.

In fact, I would say that most moms who come to me only see the negative in these reports, and that's when I see overwhelm and shut down with my clients. And why not? What you're reading in black and white becomes the picture of your child. It becomes your new reality. Then you get the diagnosis or the evaluation, and this reality only becomes darker if your mindset is not in a place where you're able to say, "Okay, this is not who I am going to accept my child to be." Of course, this thinking can also be controversial to people who think that by saying this, we are not embracing the essence of the child, of who they are. This is actually not how I advise people to deal with it. When a professional hands you a piece of paper, however, saying this is what your child tests at and this shows how they'll perform academically in certain areas, it's important to keep in mind that this is their perception of the child across one spectrum. Even if the teachers observed in an evaluation that your child doesn't get along with peers or often sits alone and is despondent, these are still observations and perceptions created for you by an outside person. They're not trying to be mean; they're doing their job. It is easy to transfer the blame to the person telling us the bad news because we often do not see our children that way. But I know for me, I was grateful for the information. I was grateful, and I needed it to know what to do next. I just could not accept everything these evaluations said.

It comes back to a theme that is pervasive among the moms I work with and, really, throughout raising children that have differences. That theme is the feeling of always having to fight for our kids. These evaluations hit like a ton of bricks, every three years. I made a decision early on to not let someone else's perception in black and white alter my own perception of whom I know my child to be. It was not going to be the truth for my child, at least not the way I saw it. Whenever Skyler or

Thomas were tested and I would get the results back, I always went to an idealistic place as a parent, setting expectations and walls that I believed may or may not be broken. I had the opportunity recently to sit in on a meeting for a client's child, the team involved were shocked at how the child's academic ability far exceeds his IQ. His mother is a huge advocate and pushes him past his own ability; if she accepted his score and believed he was below average, he would not be where he is.

I chose to create a positive perception that focused on their strengths, goodness, character, and how they were going to navigate a world that often times I felt they may not fit into. We know the truth of the world we live in, where it's often the survival of the fittest, so how are these kids that have everything against them on paper going to succeed? They'll succeed if the person that's the head of their ship, their mother and father, believes in them. I was a stay-at-home mom, and I was with Skyler and Thomas day in and day out, feeding them subliminal messages that I had hope. Yes, I read the reports, but as Skyler herself will tell you, I never, ever believed everything that was said she would or wouldn't do. I never believed there were things Skyler wouldn't do. I never allowed myself to see Skyler as a child who will struggle with cognitive rigidity her whole life because cognitive rigidity does not sound positive to me. I never even brought that term up to her until she was transitioning to her senior year. By that time, she went to her evaluation on her own. She had been seeing the same neuropsychologist who evaluated her when she was five, and here she was at eighteen, asking questions about her evaluation. She really wanted to know. When the report came back and pointed out cognitive rigidity, I explained it to her simply, "You know how sometimes you struggle in this class, or you struggle to handle things in certain ways? They call that cognitive rigidity. I just means that the way you mentally approach things is like you're tunnel-visioned and inflexible. But how do you see yourself?" I recall Skyler just looked at me with some confusion. Cognitive rigidity? She didn't see herself that way at all. She did not see herself that way because when I was told years before that this was how she was, I did not see her that way. I don't think she had people in her life that saw her in the negative aspect. Instead, she was surrounded by people who always told her she could do the next best thing.

One of my favorite professors in grad school used to say that to us. We'd be so worked up, doing case studies, student teaching. Becoming a teacher is the hardest journey I ever had to take, and it made me a better mother to all my children. This professor would say, "You know, Catherine, you just have to do the next best thing, just do the next best thing."

When you're looking at your child, it's crucial to see that child for who they are and not let someone else's perception change your perception of your child. We all have idealistic expectations. It's human nature. I'm grateful that I've always seen things in a very positive light. I was born into this world believing all things are possible and embracing faith. I've always focused on knowing God and knowing that through God all things are possible. Not everyone has that, and that doesn't hold value for everyone, and I know people who aren't spiritual at all yet they are just as positive as me. But for me, the way I tap into positivity is my faith in Jesus Christ. Knowing and creating an environment where my children know that I really *see* them, and I can look at Skyler, Katie, Vivianne, and Thomas and say, "This is my child, and this is who they are, and that's good. There's not a mistake in this. This is what I've been dealt, and it could always be worse." When I allow my perception to go down a dark path, then my children may not get the perception that they can be amazing and live a life they love.

CHAPTER 9

Mission Importance

My belief and my perception for my children and their ability to do amazing things started with really seeing them for who they were. This was the first step to creating a purpose-driven call to action, a no-holds-barred map and guide of how can I help them get from Point A to Point B.

I had a friend in college who used to always tell me, "Catherine, we want to take the path of least resistance." Sometimes I don't even know that it's possible because life is about resistance. Life is about the peaks and valleys. What I realized is I needed a plan in order to navigate and help my kids end up with that ultimate finish line, whatever that's going to be in their life. They're going to live so much more life beyond my years and my hope is to set them up to follow a system and follow a plan, to get them where they need to be.

Most of us have created a plan in our lives that allowed us to arrive at our desired outcome. The first day of graduate school, they gave us a plan, mapping out the curriculum for the full three years. So then, in my mind, I was going to become a teacher. Then circumstances led me to leave the classroom because it was just too much for my family and it was hard. I felt like I couldn't help the parents that I wanted to help. I loved helping the kids, but I couldn't reach the parents because I was so drained with the everyday rigors of being a teacher. It's such hard work. I had to make a decision to be brave and take a bold step. I sat down with my husband, who's seen me and knows my grandiose ideas. I'm more of a dreamer, and he's more logical. I said to him I wanted to start a business. I explained I was going to coach women and help them navigate the journey of raising children with disabilities. I also wanted to stay engaged in special education consulting, helping struggling learners academically. I wanted to help moms and their children through the issues that they're going to face both personally and academically and the issues that they don't even know they're going to face.

My husband just looked at me and said, "Bring me your business plan, and I'll take a look at it and see what we can personally invest to help this business to grow." At first, I thought it was his way of saying he didn't support me. But the truth was, he was bringing the reality to my dream. I stepped out, put a shingle on my office space, started my book. It's the same with helping your children navigate their lives; they have to have a plan. Ultimately, how you develop that plan is by looking at the child and seeing what they're good at and what the endpoint looks like.

For us, we started when Skyler was still really young. She developed a really amazing musical talent from a young age. We could tell, too, that she was not talking and not always making sense in conversation. It was a struggle for her. We tried to engage in conversations with our tiny girl, and she just couldn't keep up. It was hard because we didn't realize the social deficits and the struggles she was having as a child with autism and we didn't know for several years just what we were dealing with. But I could see her response to music. I would hear from teachers they were witnessing a musical ability that was beyond what a lot of her peers could do. Earlier in the book, when I talked about making comparisons to other kids, well, this was an opportunity where other people looked at Skyler and would comment, "Oh, my gosh! She can sing." That started to happen through school. In first grade, she was picked by her choir teacher to do a solo. This was the first time somebody outside of the family really acknowledged her talents. Both my husband and I knew Skyler was good, but we also knew we both loved her no matter what. I mean, everybody thinks their ugly baby is beautiful, right? This external opinion convinced us that she was, in fact, a good singer.

We started getting inklings into what Skyler's gifts and talents were. I think that's key when developing the mission for your child. Your child may not quite be able to define her purpose and develop her own life plan for herself. So again, mom is the guide. In my case, I started listening to what her gifts and talents were and noting what she clearly could not do. I would go pick her up from school, and I would have the teacher meet me at the door and tell her, "She struggled today with this or that." Or I would pick her up from a soccer practice or something and see the anxiety on her face. The coach would be nice, but I would know Skyler struggled. When it came to music, however, there was never a struggle. In music, she was the leader of the pack. She's the best at this. She had an amazing talent. Sometimes, when we are dealing with our child's disability, we may be the only person that sees that special something. In Skyler's case, her talent was clear to everyone.

Thomas's talents are manifesting themselves in ways that we're seeing but have not yet been brought to our attention by others. Thomas struggled through different sports, and, as he entered middle school, a situation presented itself. For Thomas, entering middle school meant he could now try out for sports. He is a big kid, not a heavy kid, but tall—a big guy. At fifteen, he is already 6'2", bigger than his daddy! He's 185 pounds. He is built stacked and ready to go play football. As we talked about his different options, we discovered he didn't really like football and didn't want to play football. The middle school we entered Thomas in was faith-based, where God is an integral part of their foundation for learning. When my husband called the coach, who is a great guy, and said, "Listen. This is my kid's picture. He has autism and this is what he looks like and he had struggles," the coach replied, "Hey, bring him out. This is about fellowshipping. At the school, this is what we are about. Bring him out. We welcome him. We want him to be one of the guys."

We decided to have Thomas try football, with my husband telling him he was going to love it. The first night of practice, I talked to Thomas about going, and he just looked at me and started crying. "I just need you to accept me for who I am," he said. We were faced with looking at what our mission for him had become—what we thought it should be versus the reality of what he wanted. We told him he would have to do something. Thomas explained to his father that football was not something he wanted to do. We heard him because we were the only ones who could see. It was different with Skyler. Skyler had a noticeable, audible talent that was indisputable, and we knew. For Thomas, he's tried to find that thing, and we just assumed that because of his size, it would be football. No one else was guiding us with him. No one else saw evidence of his talents. We didn't know.

He landed in cross-country running, and he's done well. He runs well, a couple times he even beat his time from the meet before, and, best of all, we found his place to shine. His important mission in his middle school years seemed to be running. Skyler's important mission is singing.

These activities have helped Skyler and Thomas navigate

the path to their own unique success stories. It's really the way I have approached any situation I have ever faced with them. We always had to have a plan, and the plan was going to tap their strengths. Often the focus with these kids is on what they cannot do. In the reports, Individualized Education Plans (IEPs) or evaluations, on the first page is the child's profile and everything that describes the child. I have moms asking me to review these for them, and many times the teacher has filled it in with their observations as well. This is the kind of the plan that is used to educate your child, but as a parent, nobody gives you that clear-cut plan to raise your child.

It's important to focus on what your child's call to action might be. We have all this information of what our kids struggle with, but what are their strengths? How can we turn these strengths into something they feel really good about? What we chose to do when we embraced Skyler's singing was immerse her in opportunities to find success in that arena. She started in first grade with the choir. We found music therapy. Fast forward 10 years, and she's now majoring in music therapy. She shared her gift, and we planted seeds. As a parent, that mission of importance is to plant those seeds of success. Skyler started with music therapy then went to vocal lessons, then volunteered with the music therapist who allowed her in there to see the other kids with autism that couldn't speak. Skyler was able to work with them and say, "Here I am, a young teenager with autism, and I'm going to work with these kids that don't speak, and I'm going to get to experience this and find success." Skyler kept experiencing dabbles of success through music. This is a kid who articulated to me from a young age, and I was willing to listen and open my ears to what her mission would be. She said to me, "Mom, I think in music. I see music notes, and I think in music. I don't really know what love feels like, but I think in music." She loves music, and no matter what happens or if she changes her major and decided to work in music ministry in her church, she has tapped into this calling.

For Thomas, we've dabbled in different things. He didn't like football in middle school. He is now entering his freshman year of high school and has decided to play football, it's amazing that he has decided to do this. I've found that I've had to be able to hear and see and open my eyes to what my children's strengths were and as I found out, I was able to create an action plan. Even if the plan at time was to let them bow out of an activity, eventually if it's meant to be, they will find their way back to it. Now, I am committed to finding avenues to help them define their mission and make it possible for them to shine.

> "Nothing is impossible, the word itself says possible." -Audrey Hepburn (Source - http://ThumbPress. com/15-awesome-inspirational-quotes-by-celebrities-and-famous-people/audrey-hepburn-3/)

CHAPTER 10

It's Okay To Be Uncomfortable

As we all know, life isn't smooth sailing. Something I realized along the way is that there are a lot of moments that challenge me as a parent. When I reflect on the journey, there have been a lot of moments that were awkward, uncomfortable, and tearful. Moments where as a parent I felt mean because I had to do things to set my kids in directions that made me question myself. Often, I had to second guess whether it was the right thing to do. I don't think parents ever stop doing that, to be honest. But I think a common thing that I see among parents who get an official diagnosis and find out their child has a disability is that then they want to go easy on them.

I've seen this often, with the kids that I've tutored or kids in the classroom. Often the parents want to excuse certain things the kid is doing or not doing. I've done it myself on occasion. We say things like, "Well, he may have lashed out because he has anxiety," or "Her behavior is a function of the disability." We don't want to push our kids into anything that will hurt them or stretch them. Obviously, when you work with professionals, you know the limits your kids have and you know what's safe for them. But as a parent, often we guard and protect them and we don't challenge them to do things because we don't want to add any more to their already full plate.

When Skyler was growing up, despite her innate musical abilities, it was all she could handle to do voice lessons. I would ask her if she wanted to take piano, and her response was always, "No. No. No. No. No. No. No. I don't want to do that. I don't want to do that." It was a real fight, so I gave up. Then she came back to me as a high school student saying, "I'm planning on majoring in music, and my piano skills are poor." She was ready to take lessons later, yet prior to that, it was clear that was one area I wasn't going to push—her or myself—to get her into. There were other areas along the way where I saw I would have to challenge her, however.

A principal wrote a little note at the end of the school year once, to another one of my daughters. These were little handwritten notes, sent to kids in the school to inspire them and encourage them and make sure they're on the right path. On this particular note, the principal had written, "It's okay to be uncomfortable because when we are uncomfortable, we grow." Once I began my work with different moms and coaching them around issues that were going on with their children, a common way in which I push my clients is to say, "Have you allowed this child to be uncomfortable?"

Discomfort allows for growth. I started small with Skyler, when she was three. She was so afraid, and we didn't know anything except the little glimpses of things that she may have been struggling with. I tried to get her to do swimming lessons, and I had to drag her, literally, kicking and screaming to swim lessons. It got to the point where my husband and I had to meet about it and determine which one of us would handle the swimming lesson. Fortunately for me, I was seven months pregnant so I easily got out of swimming lesson duty for Skyler.

We tried all kinds of things to get Skyler to swimming. She wanted a Mary Poppins video, so we tried to convince her with that. I was pushing Skyler, not knowing her limitations. It was like blind ignorance. I couldn't say she can't swim because she has anxiety, or ADHD, and all these things, because I didn't know that. Looking back, it wasn't bad parenting. I was just pushing her. I was pretty firm in the fact that she needed to learn how to swim. But it really wasn't about swimming. It was about creating the spirit of resilience. I didn't want her to give up. Don't get me wrong, there are appropriate times to let your child stop something. This wasn't one of them. As a parent, you have to gauge that. You know your child. You know when it has become too uncomfortable.

But this wasn't one of those situations. She got through it, and every week when we would take her, we'd let her know she was closer to getting her Mary Poppins video. She had a goal.

In first grade, we tried Skyler with horseback riding lessons. She thought she wanted to do it, so we did, and she didn't like is as much as she thought. So we stopped. She had that opportunity. Then, we participated in mother and daughter campouts. She usually wanted to go to those, even though she knew she would be uncomfortable because she never knew whom she was going to sleep beside. There were lots of social situations that were a stretch for Skyler. But we knew there were different things she needed to try, so we kept trying them.

We tried a social group. I took her to a social group, and although the group was made up of children with a variety of disabilities, all of them presented with a lack of social skills that required intervention. We went into this group with the speech therapist, and Skyler was with a group of kids where everyone was different. Some of the behaviors shocked her. Of course, she may have had behaviors that shocked some of the kids too. We finished the eight-week course. I remember sitting in each group and after we got home I would just want to cry, every time.

A lot of what made my kids uncomfortable made me uncomfortable. Although it made me uncomfortable, I knew she had to do it and I was trying to model that I trusted the professional who had given her the diagnosis and gave us the plan. There would be things I'd have to do for her that I wouldn't want to do, just like there would be things she'd have to do that she didn't want to do. We were in it together.

I'm always amazed at how many parents actually don't try things. I will offer suggestions to the moms I coach, things for them to try, only to have them call back a year later and hear that they never tried one of them. To me, when a professional gave me a list of things to do, I kept on the course or at least explored recommended interventions or activities to help my children. Nobody guaranteed that this was going to be pleasant, and you can't guarantee that for your child. The problem I see with the moms who don't try these things is they end up wondering why their child is coming home in tears every night. It's hard to hear that we as parents could be contributing to the tears are child cries because we are not allowing them to experience life's natural pain. We have to get okay with being uncomfortable. We have to find those situations where the professionals and others in our lives are suggesting the course we need to take and we feel resistance. That's how we know. We get an inner stirring when we know it isn't the best. It comes from a heart place. It's a heart place where as a parent, your heart is broken every time you have to make your child feel uncomfortable. It's so hard, but actually that discomfort is what empowers your children to exceed limitations that are going to hold them back as they transition into middle school, high school, and into college.

My brother held a position as a school counselor at a major university, and he was always amazed by the number of kids he'd see in the counseling center their freshman year, coming in with situations that had been unaddressed. The parents never knew what was going on. Knowing what I know now, I bet a lot of times the parents have that inner stirring, that feeling where reality was looking different but they couldn't or didn't want to embrace it. There are times that I have been brought to my knees facing issues with both of my children, and I wish some of the parents had been equipped with resources to help their kids. These kids end up going to the counselor centers as freshmen in college, depressed, and even suicidal, because the very people that were expected to figure out what their problem were for them maybe chose to ignore it or were unable to find answers. Ignoring it does not make it go away. All too often, it becomes a crisis.

I've been blessed with this opportunity to be able to talk to Skyler, my now adult daughter, and ask, "Is there anything that as I'm writing my book, I can help people with?" One thing Skyler said was, "You know, you really pushed me and encouraged me. You made me believe I can do anything, to the point that you even made me finish the things I just didn't want to do. Then when I was done, you always gave me the freedom not to go back to that particular activity or that particular group. Had I not done these things, I wouldn't have made the decision to move away from home and pursue being an independent young adult." Skyler is able to vocalize that. Sure, she still calls me asking for advice when in a tough situation. I've always encouraged her to not run from being uncomfortable because as adults, we're uncomfortable. How many of us could say that we're not uncomfortable in adult interactions socially? I'm uncomfortable sometimes. But I continue to challenge myself.

Writing this book has been uncomfortable for me. I'm putting myself out there. I've sat on a ledge for six years, not wanting to jump off, but I was telling my children the whole time to be uncomfortable. I think we live in a society where we have a net that's underneath us. All of us want this net. When our kids leave something at home, as moms we jump in the car and bring it to them. Creating a relationship where we do not let them fail, and they know it. I've done that. Many of us do that—it's what we do—but when we do this, we remove the consequences of being uncomfortable from our kids. We have to allow our kids the chance to slip through the net. The holes in the net are there to create resilience and strength that can make these kids unstoppable.

I enjoy teaching children with learning differences and disabilities more than typical kids, particularly because they have this resilience. When I am around them, they make me want to be better. They make me come home inspired. I am always inspired when I tutor or work with these kids. They're just amazing human beings that most of us can learn something from. They live in the uncomfortable and are far stronger than many of us can ever imagine.

CHAPTER 11

It's Time For School: Your Child's Education

As parents, when we transition our kids to kindergarten, we have to make a decision around which academic setting will be best for them. Really, this applies to all kids, but for parents of children with disabilities, it seems to be a bigger decision.

With Skyler, we did not even have an official diagnosis until fourth grade, and in fact, most children with disabilities are often not diagnosed until they're in a school system. It is easy to feel guilty that we didn't pick a certain school to start with, but we have to let ourselves off the hook for that.

The reality is, unless your child was diagnosed around age three or four, you really won't know there's anything different about them as they enter kindergarten. They may be starting to read and write their name, but in the preschool years, they are not yet on the academic path. They're still learning the foundations, learning to play. They're learning social skills. So it's easy not to notice any learning issues before they start kindergarten.

What we saw for Skyler in kindergarten was that she was on the periphery. She did not want to engage in the learning process. The teacher would say things to me like, "Skyler does not seem to enjoy the kindergarten experience." Of course, Skyler was my oldest, so I didn't know what the teacher meant by this at all. I had no idea what the "kindergarten experience" was! Now that I am an educator myself, I know I would never offer that kind of feedback to a parent. But those were the tips we got from Skyler's early teachers.

The comments I received about Skyler in kindergarten, that she was not processing things, or not writing letters the right way, still did not lead to anything conclusive. I felt as though Skyler was beginning to do fine and starting to perform at an average level as she was approaching first grade. As she transitioned to first grade, the school recommended Skyler participate in a summer reading intervention program with a handful of students. The program was only a week or two and was a way to build skills for students that appeared to be struggling with reading. At the time, I felt like she was going to be okay; we were getting her the help she needed, and it was going to balance out.

Ordinarily, specific learning disabilities in children are identified at school age, and most children learn to read in kindergarten. Skyler's early struggles were manifesting in ways that weren't about learning to read or count, however. For Skyler, struggle showed up in her social skills, her inability to notice her surroundings, and her poor executive functioning skills. Executive functioning relates to how we pay attention, as well as how we organize and plan, remember things, and prioritize. Executive functioning affects how we accomplish tasks throughout the day, across many levels. This is a common area of struggle for many kids with diagnoses, yet one that is not always so obvious to see in children as the signs look different across each age group.

When your child starts school, the best advice I have is to really be open to listening to what the teachers are saying. As parents, we have to be willing to open our ears and our hearts to the information we're given. All of us have emotional time-lines where we are or are not ready to hear things. For me, in Thomas's case, I remember my heart opening as he was struggling in his preschool. I started to see that things were just not right with him. He was delayed in potty training, not engaging with his peers, struggling with his letters. All of this was noticed before he even began formal schooling.

School is where the full development of the individual—social, emotional, physical, intellectual, and spiritual—begins. Little things were manifesting themselves for Skyler early on. There were gaps in her academic achievement, and she struggled with extreme anxiety. Noticing all these little things showed me that my daughter was really struggling on multiple levels. She did not know where she was at times as she navigated the playground. She did not have any sense of self-awareness. Many of these kids are unaware of things around themselves, how they are and who they are. A common trend I've noticed among the kids I work with, whether I've tutored or taught them, is that they have all struggled with aspects related to their executive functioning, like paying attention, self-awareness, and keeping themselves organized. These deficits are still evident in both Thomas and Skyler, and we continue to find strategies to help them.

Some parents pull their kids out of school upon a discovery like this and choose to homeschool. In our case, I knew I had Skyler in the right setting. She was in the right place. I knew that Skyler's first grade teacher had come from a public school and had a specialized background. I knew she knew her stuff. Knowing this, I was willing to hear her.

The question for most parents becomes: "How do you then get your child ready for school, once you have this pages-long report from a neuropsychologist outlining their diagnosis?

Is there one school that will fit all that?" For Skyler, we had four diagnoses along with autism. That's four different things going on. That's a lot to think about! Once my heart was open to hearing her teacher, I heard what her teacher saw as an issue. Skyler's teacher saw her inability to focus, being unaware of her surroundings, and not understanding what was being told to her. At least once we got the diagnosis we were able to get the school to wrap around the individual of Skyler. Skyler as the individual, with all the different things she struggled with. It's a high expectation for a teacher, with eighteen kids in her class, to hone in and focus on Skyler. As a result, Skyler's elementary teacher did not really address the issues she saw until the spring of her first grade year because it took her all that time just to get to know Skyler amid her seventeen other classmates. I had to acknowledge that the school Skyler was in might not be the right place after all. The beauty of where we had her, though, was that once we were equipped with the information and could develop a plan for the school, then we could really decide whether or not it was the right place. Most mothers don't realize that when they're navigating this decision; they think one school will fit all, only to realize that often red flags come up after they get their child in the system. These red flags are going to come along at each grade level, each step they take. For us, with Skyler, she went into second grade and did really well. It was a different dynamic, a different teacher. When Skyler was in third grade we noticed more social issues arising. She often misinterpreted the social cues of peers. She would think people didn't like her if if they looked at her in the wrong way.

What most parents also fail to realize is that the academic content only becomes greater as the child passes from third grade and up. So a child might do fine in first and second grade, but by fifth grade they're falling apart. This is because the academic expectations are higher. So now we have to bring that child to that level.

As you approach getting your child ready for school, be aware that no school year looks alike. From elementary to middle, middle to high school, and all the transitions you have, they are always different. It is really helpful to be open to talking to other parents. You can often get a lot of information from other moms around you. If you have a child struggling with dyslexia and are in a school where their needs aren't being met, listening to the experiences of other mothers might help guide your transition to a school that's a better fit.

One thing I wish I had paid more attention to with Skyler, and Thomas, too, when they were preschoolers was how they were learning at home. Of course, hindsight is 20/20, but knowing what I know now, I wish I had paid attention to their learning method that helped them each be successful. Thomas in particular. Because he presented with differences like Skyler did, I thought he would be the same as Skyler. But boys are just so different than girls, and Thomas was different than Skyler. Not having any other boys, I didn't know what to expect, but I noticed when he was three or four, he was different. So with Thomas, we had that red flag even before he entered school; it took him so long to potty train. Also, in preschool he was so behind academically. I sought out a special tutor for him recommend by a local school for children with learning differences. I remember after his first session with him, I thought she looked discouraged; it really scared me. Skyler had been able to survive, and that's what she did, all the way up until grade four when she got her official diagnosis. She wanted to be like other kids, so she would push herself and overcompensate for some of her abilities. For Thomas, his issues seemed more pervasive and in your face. It couldn't be ignored. What I observed was that the difference between a boy and girl, plus their unique personalities, meant they painted two very different pictures.

Preschool is often a child's first exposure to school, so looking at their peers as well as their siblings and asking yourself whether their behavior seems normal is part of the parent experience. Looking at other children's development was my thermometer to measure how Thomas was doing. Was Thomas at fifty degrees when he needed to be at eighty degrees? If I had paid attention to how he was engaging and learning, I would have seen he wasn't interested in learning at all. At the end of preschool, I was told he couldn't return to the Montessori he had attended, so I hired a team of people to help. Thomas had tutoring in the afternoon, a private tutor I paid to come into his new preschool. It was all a real eye opener, having other people around me looking at his learning style. I kept comparing it to Skyler's, expecting it to be where she was, but his looked different than hers. So I really had to look at Thomas as a unique being, as well as look at the other kids and gauge whether his development was age-appropriate.

Being aware of how your children are learning before they get to kindergarten age will help immensely as you decide which school to enter them into. The things you pick up from watching other kids, or your children, interacting in preschool and even on play dates are all clues. Your children are learning everyday and everywhere they go at that age. Paying attention to both what they're learning and how they're learning helps you attune to your child as a parent, and gives you a glimpse of what they need when it comes time for school.

CHAPTER 12

Navigating An Individualized Education Plan

My children attend a private school, so Skyler and Thomas started out with what was called an Alternative Education Plan (AEP). They eventually received an Individualized Education Plan (IEP) through our public school system.

When Skyler entered school, I remember being surprised that there even was such a thing. Our school was always quite progressive in the area of special education, even back in the early 2000's when Skyler entered kindergarten. They were able to notice Skyler wasn't learning like other children. For Skyler, her alternative education plan was a way for the school to see her as an individual and make accommodations that would enable her to learn in the least restrictive environment. We were lucky that we chose a private school that was willing to work hard to meet the needs of students with disabilities. I did not initiate the process of getting her help; it was her teachers who really noticed she was struggling and brought it to my attention.

Once Skyler was diagnosed in fourth grade, we knew that school was only going to be more challenging with each coming year. It was already obvious that the difference between Skyler and her peers was greater. I liken it to a ladder with twelve rungs. Skyler was stuck on the 6th rung, while around her were kids on the 8th, 9th, even 12th rungs. With Skyler's official diagnosis came more specific individualized accommodations that fell under a realm of disabilities making her eligible for an IEP.

Due to the fact that Skyler was in a private school, the process of getting an official IEP started with her diagnosis from a neuropsychologist. Ordinarily, in a public school, a school psychologist administers the assessments found in the Evaluation Team Report (ETR). The process is normally either initiated by a parent or a school official. In the state we reside, in order for Skyler to be eligible for a state scholarship, she needed to have an IEP through our public school district of residence. In order to be eligible for an IEP, the child has to have a diagnosis that falls in one of the 13 categories under the Individuals with Disabilities Education Act (IDEA), and the disability has to have a negative effect on a child's ability to learn. If a child does not qualify for an IEP, they may be eligible for a 504, a plan that provides services and or changes to learning environment for students with learning and attention issues.[1]

Regardless of which plan it is, once it is in place, goals for the child are outlined based on their unique disability. The goals and objectives indicated on an IEP are designed to target the specific area the student needs help in (reading, math, writing), and the student's progress is monitored. Parents will normally receive a progress report every nine weeks so they are aware of the progress their child is making. For instance,

---

[1]   For more information on the difference between the IEP and the 504 plans, visit https://www.understood.org/en/school-learning/special-services/504-plan/the-difference-between-ieps-and-504-plans

Skyler struggled with reading so she had a goal in place that said when Skyler read, she had to use a variety of strategies to address her reading comprehension deficit by being able to answer literal/inferential questions with 90 percent accuracy. Every nine weeks, when I received data on this goal, I could track and see if what we were doing was working. This was a beautiful thing for Skyler—and Thomas as well—as I was able to see them meet the goals set out in their plans. The IEP is reviewed on an annual basis.

It's helpful to find the resources and support you need when it comes to understanding an IEP. I had no prior education in that area and I became passionate about understanding. I came out of college with a journalism degree and Skyler's report was twenty pages! I remember sitting through these meetings, year after year, looking at this IEP and feeling very overwhelmed. As I have been working with parents over the last several years, I find they feel most overwhelmed with the IEP process. When they get a report on their child identifying all the issues he or she has, and it comes with all these recommendations, often they don't understand what it means.

Really, though, the IEP is your child's golden ticket. An IEP is so beneficial to your child. It's the plan of how they're going to learn. Reading through Skyler's IEP helped me to understand that the plan is in place to address the holes. The psychologist once explained to me that Skyler's brain was like Swiss cheese, that there are a lot of these little holes, and you never know when the holes will come up. With an IEP, we are now filling the holes. When we identified Skyler's holes, the goals were to help her get higher up on the ladder. Once we identified that, we were able to help her start the climb.

I think it would surprise people to read that here I am, writing a book, yet when Skyler was young, I had paper after paper in front of me, and I didn't understand them. I'm married to a physician who is also very educated, and he didn't understand them either! I really wanted to understand, so when I decided to pursue my master's in special education, it wasn't because I wanted to be a teacher. I was tired of going into education plan meetings for two children and not knowing what was going on. Now that I know what's going on, I help others interpret IEPs, 504's, and ETRs It's amazing how much the average parent doesn't know.

Now I look at the goals in my kids' plans and challenge the team. I'm not trying to be adversarial, but I am taking an active interest in the education of my children. So when I ask a teacher if Skyler has met a goal and they report that she met it with 90 percent accuracy but Skyler tells me different, I want to know where the discrepancy lies. On a team, everybody wants your child to succeed. I would have no idea what was going on at these meetings and would sometimes just nod my head despite feeling clueless. Once I began the process of pursuing my master's, I came equipped with questions.

The sad reality is, however, to truly understand these plans, you need a licensed intervention specialist to help you. I empowered myself and went back to school, and that's not realistic, nor should it be necessary. Make sure you understand and ask questions. Ask the team of teachers in the room. I didn't do that because I didn't know what to challenge. As you navigate the IEP, it's okay not to know, but ask questions because it shouldn't be necessary to have a degree in special education just to understand your child's IEP.

Over time, the education for your child changes, and the level of demands put on the students gets more intense each year. The expectations and the way children with disabilities see their peers perform are so stressful. If you're trying to get your child to read at a fifth grade level, by the time they gradu-ate high school, everything is getting harder, whether they're in the resource room or the general education classroom.

We have to embrace the fact that education changes over time. Children's needs and accommodations are going to change over time; they'll get better at some things and worse at some things. I wasn't prepared for Skyler, who graduated with straight A's, to go to college and struggle. I thought college would be easy for her. It's been easy in some ways, but there are still holes. Realize as education changes over time, you have to continue to ask questions along the way, and by the time your child is a senior in high school, you might get what's going on. Unless you have a special education degree or you're a princi-pal, you won't understand fully, and you shouldn't be expected to understand.

There's also a different team every year. Some teams are more willing to spell it out than others, but if you continue to ask the questions and you're invested, it's going to pay off for the child. Education itself is unique and different every year. It is also differentiated to the human being; it's never going to look the same for any two children. It's okay to ask questions. Most teachers really like to know parents are invested. One of the principals who worked with my kids said, after my son went through, "I wish there were more parents like you." Sure, we don't often feel like our kids are the role models—when they have all the issues, and we're just surviving getting them through each grade—but even before I became a licensed teacher, I never felt like my job was to harass teachers into educating my child. I always took a stake in their success and made sure that if I didn't know the answer, I'd find it. I always asked people around me to help me. It's always possible, and the person who benefits the most is the child on the IEP.

CHAPTER 13

My Child Is Alone

O ne of the most difficult things I have found in raising children with disabilities and coaching moms is that these kids often don't have any friends. There's no way to sugarcoat this; they are often socially isolated. For a lot of moms, it doesn't seem like it will get any better. It can be really hard, because as moms we often want to fix everything for our children.

I've shed a lot of tears about this through the years. As I followed my children from elementary to junior and high school, I would see these amazing little humans. I saw they were so kind and sweet, and I could not understand how someone couldn't love them. Why wouldn't everyone want to be their friend? I think this is the most difficult thing to watch. It seems to be kind of universal, that often these kids that are developmentally behind their peers don't have the social skills to keep up with them. I have a unique perspective because I am raising two kids that don't have disabilities and therefore don't struggle as much socially and I have two kids that do. At the end of Skyler's last year of elementary school, I realized that she hadn't been invited to any birthday parties. When I compared this to Vivianne, my second daughter, who was always being invited places, I could see the huge disparity. Because she was the oldest child, I didn't realize how much Skyler had been left out all those years.

Skyler was in fourth or fifth grade before I realized nobody was asking her to come over. When I would go to the playground, I would see her off by herself running around, no one talking to her. She would engage in parallel play, simply playing next to the other kids and copying them.

For me, the hardest thing about Skyler being alone was that I couldn't fix it. I volunteered at the school when Skyler was in elementary, and I specifically chose to work in the lunchroom so I could watch her. I kept that job for five years and did it again when Thomas was in school so I could make sure he was okay. It's amazing the lengths moms will go to! I used to laugh with the ladies in the lunchroom I worked with because we were all the most educated and overqualified lunch ladies in the state. We were really just a bunch of hovering moms trying to smother their children. I knew Katie and Vivianne were fine. I looked around the room and could see that Skyler wanted to be around people, but no one would sit with her. Thomas didn't seem to care about being around people. It wasn't about what my wish for them was; it was about what their wish for themselves was. I would look at Skyler, and I knew she didn't want to be alone, while Thomas didn't care, and my heart would break for Skyler.

Still, we have to be mindful of what our child's wishes are because when we try to force socialization, it never works. I tried to force socialization with Thomas, and he would often tell me he wasn't ready or it felt like too much for him. I had a dream for Skyler to be a popular girl who everyone invites everywhere, but it's been a struggle for her. Being around people does not come intuitively for her. She doesn't understand, and it's effort and work for her to be social. At times it has been downright painful. Now that she is older, Skyler can articulate when she is drained and will find a way to take a break from people. For a lot of these kids, the social struggles are really a comorbidity of the disability. Simply put, they accompany their primary diagnosis.

As a parent, how often do you solve a problem that is often unsolvable? For me, I found that in trying to solve the social problem, the number one thing was making sure that my children felt loved at home. There were times, especially with Skyler, that I was hard on her. She would act out in ways that were normal, and I would be on her. Then it dawned on me that her home is the most comfortable place she has, so if I was hard on her at home, she didn't have anywhere to find support.

I started to give her the tools to build her sense of self. I would let her know I saw her looking lonely in the lunchroom, and I saw her decide to sit by another little girl. I'd tell Skyler I was proud of her for sitting by that girl because that girl was also alone most of the time. I had a dialogue with Skyler about what I saw. This translated into Skyler becoming a very compassionate person. Now, at 19, she has a friend in college that was totally isolated and struggling. It's funny how Skyler is now the person trying to help people that are broken. Equipping our kids with a sense of self worth allows them to know they are worth being liked and that they are loved and valued. In Skyler's situation, she was able and aware enough to see that perhaps there was a reason she struggled here.

That's the beauty of getting on the other side with your children, when they're ready for college, or entering a job, or whatever their future holds. I have continued to verbally build my children up every day and give them that sense of self worth. I saw social growth with Skyler most notably in her senior year of high school. It seemed at that point as though she understood: "I am who I am, and there are people I tried to get to like me that didn't, and it doesn't matter." She got that the people she thought she wanted to hang out with, people who were rejecting her, were maybe not the people she wanted to be with after all.

For us, it worked to have dialogue with Skyler and Thomas. It comes down to helping the child realize there are people around them that love them and that they matter. It could be in the form of spending time with them, talking to them, giving them nonverbal affection. Sometimes that's the only way I felt I was making a difference for Skyler and Thomas.

Of course, Thomas didn't care about engaging socially, and there are lots of kids like that. It's our job as parents to make them realize they need people. When you have a child rejecting socialization and they don't want friends, how do you make them realize they want people? With Thomas, I had to remind him that he was going to be a person functioning in the world of people. He was going to have a job, and he had to learn to get along with people. Now that he is in his mid-teens I have to remind him that he has to "man-up." I will remind him that one day he, too, will have a family and he'll be the big man. That he cannot just stay at home and not be out in the world around people. I had to let him know that being around people may not always be a choice he wants to make, but it's a necessity. I told Thomas that he was a valued and needed part of the world, and I was not going to give him a free pass because he was autistic and had a social disorder. I even told him once, "I need you need to be part of this world because you're too amazing not to be."

Often, when our kids are struggling and we see them all alone, we want to solve it and create friendships for them. The truth is, the biggest friendship they need to solve is with themselves and family first. They need to love themselves. I threw

Skyler into all kinds of social groups, and they were valuable, but in some ways they made her feel more different. Sometimes for Skyler, being in an organized social group made her feel like there was more of a problem than she thought there was. Skyler noticed that sometimes in the groups the others were struggling so much more than her, and it made her feel weird. I had to be willing to listen, and to understand that I wasn't going to help her find friends by throwing her in a group of kids where she felt worse. It was the same for Thomas. He didn't want to go to a group full of autistic kids because he was tired of hearing about other people's problems, and he didn't see himself like the others. For both Skyler and Thomas, because they loved themselves and had strong self-worth, they were able to see that these groups weren't for them and voice that to me. We did all sorts of groups and Special Olympics, and there is a time and place for these, but when our kids were ready to stop and asked to do something different, even if it was staying home with us because that's where they felt good, we had to honor that.

As mothers, we are born nurturers and caregivers, and it's important to realize that sometimes some people say the child's disability is not about the mom. I disagree. I do think it has a lot to do with the mom. Moms take it personally, and a lot of mothers believe that they are a failure because their child has a disability. I've never felt that, but I did feel it was my job to ensure my kids had everything better than I did and that they were not going to struggle. I felt responsible that they didn't have friends, so I started creating opportunities for them to make some. For Thomas, these opportunities often made him uncomfortable, and I made him persevere through the discomfort anyways. When a child is alone socially, a lot of it has to do with how they feel about themselves and their ability to be social. Having a social disability is really hindering; there is so much that's not natural, so asking our kids to "just go make friends" doesn't work. They have no idea what to do.

I've tried different interventions for both Skyler and Thomas. With Thomas, we started Relationship Development Intervention or RDI, where he has worked on strategies to tap into his dynamic intelligence, which is not intuitive for him. This was a parent-directed initiative and a relatively new thing. It's teaching him the tools that will allow him to thrive on his own. I throw him into uncomfortable situations, but I make sure he can handle it.

We were also in a class where we practiced making phone calls to people. I had to find people he could call, and he would have to practice getting on the phone and having conversations. I remember how hard it was to ask people if their sons could accept a call from Thomas. At times, I hated the class because I did not want to ask if my son could call someone's son. I remember feeling really selfish for feeling that way, Thomas had it way harder than I did, but looking back, it was hard on me as well. I often gave myself a hard time feeling this way. Most of my friends were not having to do anything like this; their kids could just make phone calls, and mine had to be trained. In retrospect, I should have let myself off the hook for feeling bad.

Now in college, Skyler pledged a sorority in her first year. Here I had a kid who struggled through elementary and high school, who went to college and sought out pledging a sorority! She was confident to do it and also navigated it all herself. Beyond that, however, I continued to put them in uncomfortable situations, and that's really what allowed for growth. Skyler has since transferred to another university that is closer to home. She informed me that she was going home with another student for the weekend of fall break. A friend of mine asked if I was mad she wasn't coming home. I said, "No way! She has a friend!"

None of my kids are the most popular ever, but I never wanted that. I don't wish that upon my kids. I want them to love themselves. These are conversations I have with all four of my children: I say, "If you can define your own sense of self-worth and really love yourself, people will love you, and if they don't, then you've got to dismiss them." We believe in God and we have a faith experience and my children understand that if they believe in God they have a friendship that is never taken from them. In the end, they're never alone; they have you, developing the family unit and empowering them into loving themselves.

CHAPTER 14

Creating Your Child's Tribe

O nce your children are in school, and you start to notice the different areas where they need help, you will see the importance of creating a tribe for your children. When I think of the word tribe, I think of a group of likeminded people that have an end goal in common; that's my personal definition of tribe. That's what I wanted for Skyler and Thomas.

Most of the women I've coached have told me they want the same thing. I worked with one mom who wanted to create a plan for their child who was struggling. My first question was, "What do you want your child's life to look like?" We need to consider what we see as the end goal for the child. For this mother, she said she wanted her son to be academically and socially sound. Every parent has a goal for their child, and what I learned in my experience with Skyler and Thomas was that it was not going to be just one person that gets them to that academically and emotionally sound level I desired for them. I knew early on it would take a team of people. Often as mothers we think we can do it all, but we can't. Not only that, it's ultimately a major drain on us, trying to do it all. It also drains the child, and the marriage if you're married. Or if you're a single mother with no support, it all falls out beneath you.

When I looked at developing a tribe for my child, I looked at what steps were needed to take to get them to the goal. For the mom I was coaching, we looked at what needed to happen to get her son academically and socially sound. There were five major areas to be considered.

The first area is the child's social life. What were our goals for our children? In the case of the mother I was coaching, she told me her son didn't have any friends. We created social goals, like finding a play buddy for him at school. This meant that his mother might have to contact other mothers, be candid with them, and see if they would bring their children to play with her son. It was up to the mother at first to develop these friendship opportunities and set up playdates for her son. It's helpful when you have a child with special needs to also seek out play dates with their neurotypical peers so they have models for typical behavior. I know as we developed Thomas's tribe I've had to find people and be honest with them. I had to let them know Thomas has autism, he struggles socially, and ask if they would be willing to set up a play date. Fortunately for us, I found other mothers to do this with, and they eventually became part of my and Thomas's tribe.

Another strong tribe member can also be a speech therapist. If your child has an issue where he or she is struggling with language, a speech therapist is a huge asset to your child's team. This will help your child socially and connect you to other mothers and children who share the struggle, or at least understand your child's struggle. Often speech therapy is offered at school if a child qualifies for this related service on their IEP, of no charge to the parent. I have known parents who choose to hire a speech therapist privately if their child is not offered this service at school.

The second area is emotional support. For Skyler, there were times when she was struggling so much I felt like I needed to reach out and find a counselor, pastor, or someone willing to talk to her. Something that worked for us was finding a female college student, about four or five years older than Skyler, who was willing to spend time and be a mentor to Skyler. If you have a child that needs emotional support, it is helpful to find someone to take on the mentor role.

Keep in mind, your child's tribe is going to be people outside of mom and dad, and that's the point. For Skyler, it was a college student as mentor. For Thomas, I found a junior in high school, a big football star. He would pick Thomas up and take him out on outings. He also offered Thomas emotional and mental support. I paid this teenage boy, and he thought it was great. He didn't see it as work. You can choose to pay a teen or find a teen willing to help out as community service. In my experience, I wanted to make sure whomever I added to the tribe would be consistent, and I found that when I paid someone to work with my child and they were interested in it, they were far more consistent than if I didn't. I'm paying people to be invested, and paying them shows that I value them and their time. I've never had an issue with people canceling when I've paid them.

The third area is spirituality. I tried to find people who were of similar faith to ours when seeking a tribe member. The young man I hired to work with Thomas was also Christian and the son of a pastor. We're a Christian family, and I appreciate that he can address spiritual issues or questions Thomas might have. He's like-minded, and he understands the goals we have for Thomas, and also our family philosophy. Another advantage to being spiritually like-minded is that often when you seek a mentor from your spiritual community, teen or adult, they will want to do it as a philanthropic opportunity.

The fourth area is physical development. You might look at hiring a personal trainer to help your child. We hired a trainer to work with Thomas. He's the same gender, understands the importance of physical fitness, and he's a role model of what males do and how males can be successful. Thomas looks up to him.

As you're looking for people to work with your child, it's helpful to have good interviewing skills. You will want to know how they feel about working with someone with disabilities, or what they knew about autism or your child's unique diagnosis. Make sure you find people who understand it and are open to it, and if they don't have experience, they have a heart for children who struggle. Thomas's trainer communicates with him well and doesn't treat him differently, and that was so valuable because I needed someone who would not be afraid to tell Thomas when he was doing something inappropriate.

The fifth area is intellectual and academic. This area is about finding a team of tutors that can support your child intellectually and academically and help them reach the goals that have been set. I'm a teacher, but I do not tutor my own children. It's often better to have outside checks and balances from the team of people outside of mom. Children often don't respond to their parents as well as they do to other people. Starting when my kids were young, I've hired tutors for them, and not necessarily certified teachers, either. I have hired students that were in college or grad students, and they were more than competent. Most parents that hire me to tutor their children do so because they don't want to have a battle every day, or be the heavy. For Thomas, we have three different tutors that work with him after school. A full team! We had a different model of academic support for Skyler. Now that she is at college, she's learned to equip herself with support and find tutors, mainly older students. She sought it out herself when she started college.

Developing this team shows your children that they need support. They also see that here they have a tribe of people who want them to be successful, people outside of mom and dad. They start seeing different ways of developing success. With the support of their tribe, they become well-rounded individuals and more independent as they transition into adulthood because they've had a tribe of people to support them along the way. They also learn to become an amazing advocate for themselves, and when they see they need support they will ask for it. This is a skill in our family that has been building over time.

I constantly meet moms who want to do it all. But we just can't. Having a tribe really sets your child up for success and independence. The skills are all so varied—the physical therapist, the tutor, the mentor, the counselor, the team of teachers—yet your child's success is the common goal. Everyone on the tribe has a stake in the success of your child. We all know it takes more than one perspective to succeed, and I've seen firsthand that with multiple perspectives and repeated practice with different individuals over time, a child will develop successfully. I have tons of people in my life helping me and am grateful to have a team to help Skyler and Thomas reach their end goals. It is an essential part of the process of helping your child live a life they love.

CHAPTER 15

Balanced Living

For many women, our understanding of motherhood is based on the mothers we had and the example they set. My example was a mom who was very efficient, organized, and always got everything done, despite working full-time and having five children. She seemed to be able to manage it all.

I didn't seem to be cast from the same mold, however. I was never a Type-A person who could throw five balls in the air and juggle them all, doing everything well while I was at it. My mother represented someone who could do it all well. I never saw her fall apart. Considering how many times I fall apart in front of my kids—at least weekly—this is amazing to me. I never saw my mom lose it. She was always so together. This was my view of motherhood.

It was a beautiful experience to be mothered that way, but it also hurt me as I became a mother myself. The experience left me feeling as though I should be like my mother, and I'm not like her. I'm not wired like her. I felt a lot of guilt about this. When I would talk with my mother, particularly when I was in my early 30's, I would always ask her why it was so hard to be a mother, why I couldn't do it like she did. Of course my mother, being so kind, would remind me that she didn't have two children with such great needs as I did. She pointed out that my situation was much harder than hers, while gently reminding me not to compare.

It took my mother pointing out that my plate was really full in order for me to realize I had a lot going on and that I was okay given that I had four kids, two of whom were struggling with disabilities. The reality was I had a lot more on my plate than the average mom. It was an epiphany for me. Now, I see the moms I coach wondering why they're struggling, and I am the one reminding them of how well they're doing considering the challenge it is to have children with disabilities. I help them own the fact that raising children with special needs is hard. It's not necessarily that it's harder than raising kids who don't have disabilities, but it's certainly different. There are things we have to deal with that other people don't, and knowing and owning this fact is important. We feel like we're treading water.

We live in a world where we do a lot of comparison. Add to this that by nature I'm an insecure person, and it's no wonder I felt like I was treading water for many of my early parenting years. When we feel like we're treading water, chances are we are not living a balanced life.

Balanced living is really living a life where you're at peace in a lot of areas. For me, balanced living came from taking inventory, first and foremost of my health, my mental wellness and nutrition, and where I was at with really taking care of my body. In my faith, I view my body as a temple. Now, have I always treated it like this? Absolutely not! I have engaged in gluttonous behavior. I've done things where I'm not honoring the body I've been given. As a mother raising children with disabilities, I tended to put myself last. Not taking good care of my health really left me feeling bad about myself and perpetuated the treading water mentality. I never worried about what I was eating because I was worried about what my kids were eating.

The turning point for me came when I began my first full-time teaching job, teaching special education in a high school.

I did a health inventory; they did one for all teachers. This was a profile where they checked our bone density, nutrition, weight—everything. I knew I was overweight and that my cholesterol was high, but this profile revealed that I was also losing bone mass, meaning I'd be a higher candidate for osteoporosis. It was a big wake-up call for me. I thought I was doing well, but I was not living balanced or eating well at all. It took an outside team of people to ring my wellness bell and tell me I was not in good shape. I don't take medications and was not on any medications at the time, but had I kept going down that path, medication may have become a viable reality.

The worst, though, was that I was raising children that were looking to me as a role model and I wasn't modeling what I was telling them to do. As mothers, it's too easy to drift into "do as we say not as we do" behavior. I knew I wanted to walk the talk. I ended up leaving that teaching job. Skyler was struggling, and I became quite sick. I believe being sick had everything to do with me not living a life where I was in a healthy place. I simply wasn't taking care of my health.

I left that teaching job and quit teaching altogether. I hit the new year and decided to hire a weight loss coach. This was new to me. I had tried lots of diets but never hired a coach. The coach made a huge difference in my life. I lost almost twenty pounds. I learned to stop using my children as an excuse for not living my life fully. I have still struggled from time to time, though, and will put a few pounds on here or there, but I now know how to take them off.

I improved my nutrition and took ownership of the example I was setting for my children. I was always pretty good about my physical fitness and taking care of myself, but I also thought that as long as I worked out, I could eat whatever I wanted and not worry about it. Making this change, I committed myself to the fact that if I'm not feeding my body in a healthy way, it doesn't matter. If I eat too many calories, working out doesn't mean anything. How we eat is directly correlated with how we view our body, and it sets the foundation for living a balanced life.

If this is an area you would like to change for yourself, I encourage you to find the program that works for you. There are so many programs out there. What I loved about the wellness coach I worked with was the way she helped me set everything up based on what my needs were. I was able to discover that a lot of my issues with how I was eating were emotional and the decisions I was making about how to fuel my body had everything to do with how I felt about myself. It's easy to overlook how we feed and treat ourselves, but the truth is it goes way beyond food and calories. My wellness coached helped me find myself emotionally and tap into that.

It was a journey I couldn't have done alone. Hiring the weight loss coach was a crucial investment that I made in myself. I learned to let go of judgment, not expect myself to be my mother, and take ownership of who I am and my success. It is really easy to say we can't afford to do these things, but there are always ways. I had a friend who said she couldn't afford it, and she ended up bartering her printing services for personal training. There are always opportunities available. The truth is, we can't afford NOT to do this. Living a balanced life transcends into more success for everyone around you, especially your children. So many of the mothers I work with have told me they struggle with their body and wellness. To me, the common link is that we are pouring everything we have into our children. Yet if we do this, we end up being really unhealthy. Believe me, I know from experience. I want to leave my children a legacy of someone they're proud of. I started to feel ashamed of the message I was sending, so I did something about it. Even to this day, I don't always send them the greatest messages but I know I have one life to live. I'm not always perfect but when I see I need to make changes, I do.

What do you want your legacy to be? A life out of balance? How do you feel when you don't take care of yourself? I have grown to a point now where I am aware when I'm not practicing good self-care. I get angry with my kids; I'm not the best mother. I look at myself twenty pounds ago, and it's true; I was quicker to anger, more irritable, grumpier. I was depressed about not being my best self. I was physically not feeling good. When I started to lose weight and feel good about my nutrition and the things I was doing, I was nicer. I was a nicer mom, and this transcended into making my children better people over time. I still have a ways to go and continue to set goals for myself. Owning my physical well-being and knowing just how much it affects the kind of mother I am has shown me what's possible for parenting and has led to a far more successful childhood for my kids.

CHAPTER 16

Create Mom's Tribe

It is really common that as mothers we think of our families first and put ourselves last. But if a typical family has mom and dad at the top and then the children, it's important to recognize that as a mom, you're part of the team steering the family, and you are modeling all the time. Ideally you have a healthy relationship to model to the children, and they get to see what that looks like. This way the kids realize mom and dad's relationship has to be the primary so they can have energy to put towards the children as they set them up to go off in the world and be successful adults.

I grew up in a typical family, with two parents that loved each other and never fought. It was amazing and seems to be a rare thing now. The reality is more like we intend to have date nights or put the relationship first—or if you're a single mother, you plan to have a night out once a week—but then we do the opposite. Sometimes my husband and I don't even see each other at all by the end of the week!

The reality is that all our energy goes to taking the kids to all the events, therapy, tutoring, or sports they are involved in. Any parent today is feeding into their children so much that sometimes the end of the week comes and we realize we've been on autopilot and our other relationships have become non-existent. When my kids were little, I had a team of other moms around me who were also stay-at-home moms and we took care of each other. Now the kids are teens, and it's taken a big effort to develop that same mom tribe. All of us have older kids, which makes it hard to have the same network of support, as we are driving to more activities and caught in the hustle and bustle with teenagers. Creating that tribe of support, however, means I have a tribe of people that want to see me succeed. They're people I admire and look up to in all different areas. Having a tribe means surrounding myself with positive people that want to see me do better and not bring me down. When I began coaching, I realized I needed a coach myself, so I found a weight loss coach and a business coach and welcomed them into my tribe. I've been lucky to have different people in my life to coach me through situations. When one of my coaches once told me that I was the average of the five people I spend the most time with, it really got me thinking. Who was it that was in my tribe? I realized who they were. I was grateful to have a good mom tribe.

Developing a tribe of people is about being open. Opening our hearts to new people and opening our hearts to taking risks. By putting myself out there, I've met people who have become part of my tribe who now help me succeed and meet my goals. Opening up and developing my tribe gave me the opportunity to be blessed in other ways, including helping to make this book a reality. This book has been a journey that has lasted more than six years. Really, the stall in getting the book into print was fear. I had a very kind person that is part of my editing team remind me that too many people need inspiration to raise children with special needs. For me not to get the book done is ridiculous. Had I not had this member of my tribe, I would never have had the courage to complete this book.

Of course, creating your tribe looks different for everyone. You might make a new friend at church, or start a book club. Find people who share your interests. I took a class on how to use PowerPoint and met like-minded women there. I have a good friend developing her tribe through a running club she met on Facebook. She connects with other women in her neighborhood, and they meet to run once a week. She's developed good friendships through this. Part of her process was being discerning until she found people who were truly like-minded. It's important not to settle when it comes to choosing your tribe.

Identify who the most important people are in your life, outside of your spouse and your children. Who is the most important adult in your life and how can they be part of your tribe? What I've found for me is that definitely some of the most important friends I have do not have children with special needs. Sure, you need friendships with people whose kids struggle like yours, but you also need balance. A balanced tribe will have people in it who will speak the truth to you. Maybe they don't live in your realm of raising children who struggle, but that's okay. I have a good friend who whenever I go off into a pity party, perhaps lamenting that Skyler has no friends, challenges my thinking. She'll call me out on feeling sorry for myself and try to get me off the pity party. There are other friends I have who will engage in just saying what I want to hear, or I'll do it to them; we don't want to offend. Not having people in your life who speak truth to you is detrimental because then you're not really part of an authentic tribe.

Another member of my tribe is my personal trainer. While I have a friend I run with that doesn't cost me anything, it's not the same as having a trainer. When I go to my trainer, she tells me the truth. If I didn't eat well and I'm wondering why I didn't lose weight, she'll point out the obvious. She will look at my food log and see my bad decisions. She tells me the truth, and I can hear it and not take it personally. A year ago, I used to take these things to heart and become offended easily. I still do that sometimes, but I'm improving because I don't want a tribe of people who are going to lie to me. I want a tribe of people who will really push me to be the best I can be.

It's the same with my husband. Do I want to keep him in a place where he doesn't want me to have a nervous breakdown? I tend to be a crier, and when my husband tells me what I don't want to hear, I'll cry. I'm trying to become more resilient because I know if he doesn't speak the truth—and I can't hear the truth—we're not growing.

Having a team of people that want you to be the best you can be is really the key to being a better parent and raising children who are the best they can be. There really is a lot of truth to that old Michael Jackson song, "Man in the Mirror." If you don't have an exceptional team around you, how can you expect to become exceptional or raise exceptional children? One of the things I do when I am coaching is redirect my clients back to themselves. It seems like nobody wants to look at themselves. Often when we look at the people closest to us, we'll find that we have some dead weight, people who are really not the top five people we want to be surrounded by. When we shed that dead weight and surround ourselves with people that want us to excel—and therefore help us create children that excel—we're more willing to hire that coach or open our heart to that person that seems intimidating. The people that intimidate us often help us raise our self-esteem. Sometimes the people that most threaten us and seem intimidating are the best ones to have on our tribe.

Why wouldn't we want to draw ourselves towards women who are confident and make us want to be better? I own the fact that I want a tribe of people around me that make me want to be better, and I'm grateful to have found one.

CHAPTER 17

Embrace Your Spirituality

When I was working on my master's degree, I took an introduction to special education class. It was a basic, introductory class, but one of the lectures really caught my attention. We were working with a mainstream, secular text, but there was a section in it discussing the role of faith when raising children with disabilities. There I was in a class with a cross-section of people who believed different things, reading a mainstream text saying faith is helpful in families raising children with disabilities and plays a role in the success of the children with the disability. As a Christian, I have no doubt about the power of faith when it comes to raising children with disabilities. There's a huge correlation, and I believe my children are a great example of this.

I was raised in a Catholic home where my parents definitely lived out their faith on a daily basis. People sometimes think I am embellishing when I say that, but I assure you, I'm not. I'm the youngest of five. My mom's dream was to have five boys; the oldest was going to be named after our father, and the remaining four would be Matthew, Mark, Luke, and John. Instead, she had three boys and two girls, so she got Matthew and Mark, and my sister and I erased Luke and John. From a young age, my mother really lived caught up in the gospel and the word of God. It was the same with my father, and growing up what I saw was my parents continually opening our home to "unlikely people," people that others would often be fearful of having around their children or even themselves. There were a lot of foster children, for example.

My mother was also part of a program called Open House, a program started by her friend that sought to house pregnant teenage girls. We had some of these girls come live with us as they finished out their pregnancies. These were girls who were from small towns in Missouri and their parents didn't want anyone to know they were pregnant, so they sent them off to have the baby. Once they gave birth, the girls would return home, pretending nothing ever happened. It was all a very hush-hush situation. Throughout my childhood, we had five or seven young unwed mothers come live with us. This was in a time where people wondered why my parents would want their daughters to be around "girls like that."

It left the impression on me that my parents were serving. The local nunnery knew about my parents and would call them to help. Once we had a young woman in her 20's come, having been hidden by the nuns from an abusive lover. We hid her in our house. I gave her my room. I remember her face was black and blue and she had a wig on, and I will never forget the impression she left upon me. Another time, my parents were asked to help with taking a schizophrenic through regression therapy. I saw a 21-year-old go through bottle feedings by my parents to help her revisit her childhood wounds and heal.

Now that I'm the mom of four teens, I am amazed at the willingness of my parents to surround themselves with these "broken people" and not think twice. They truly saw the face of God in everyone they encountered. They let these people in with full faith that we would all be fine. My perspective was so different, growing up this way. I think it's just amazing that my parents did this, no questions asked, again and again. My siblings and I, for the most part, emerged unscathed from the open-door policy my parents had. There were only a few situations where we were affected (like the time a girl locked me and my sister in the closet before she stole the family car), but that was the worst of it. I don't feel I walked away viewing it as a negative thing. I saw my parents living out of their faith and embracing their faith with God, no questions asked, at any cost. Some of the situations could have gone badly, and they didn't. My mom and dad had faith, so I got to see what an active life of faith looks like.

What is faith? Believing in something we cannot see. To me, my mother, who loved us very much, choosing to bring people into our home that could have harmed us was an act of faith. The testament to her faith was the truth of the experience: none of us were harmed. My parents believed that God would protect them and us, and overall we all turned out really well. We were happy. I know that the faith I witnessed gave me a foundation to believe in that which was unseen. For me, raising children with disabilities, faith is the only way that I have gotten through some of the hurdles we've faced.

Who do we put our faith in? It's easy to put our faith in external things—money, looks, other people. There is also the idea that if we put our faith in the external we'll be happy. But it doesn't work, looking for external affirmation in different things. As I have raised my kids, I've wondered: am I giving my children what my parents gave to me? It's a process. Having kids who have the needs my kids do, we wanted to show them what faith is and put them in an environment where they know that no matter what, with God all things are possible, like the passage in the Bible, "I can do all things through Christ who gives me strength," (Phillippians 4:17). With that foundation, our children know they can look to the Lord to find the answers to questions that have no answers.

I've seen families that don't have faith and those that do, and the families who have that belief in God are able to manage their lives in a way that's peaceful. They manage with peace. They're not always happy, but they understand that with the faith experience they're moving from hopeless to hopeful. There are more days where they can draw upon their faith for help. The faith experience is important to me personally because I want to leave a legacy my children can live into. What is the biggest gift I can leave for them? Money? A book? That's not the legacy for me. Instead, having a faith that is eternal, that transcends my life when I'm gone and is something they can share with their own children; that, to me, is a powerful legacy. I encourage everyone to find their faith. For me as a Christian, the only way is through Christ. For you, it may be something else. I know everyone comes from different experiences so be willing to explore and take risks. What legacy do you want to leave?

We're often living for worldly things, all the financial accolades, yet everything we're pursuing will not be going with us to heaven. That's why it is faith I hope to leave for my children.

Perhaps because she's more mature, I've seen Skyler embracing her faith passionately as she has transitioned to high school and college. We also put her in an environment where not only did she have her faith at home, she also had an opportunity to embrace her Savior at school by being in a learning community of believers. Skyler was able to seek out her faith through different teachers, and she got to see the different ways faith can look each year with a different teacher. Now that she's gone on some mission trips, she's been able to communicate to me the fact that faith was really what helped her through some of the struggles she's gone through. She has shared with me that there was no way she could have gotten through some of her darkest times without knowing her ultimate friend is in Christ. She also made a brave decision to transfer colleges after one year so that she could be in an active Christian community. It was a bold and courageous decision for her to recognize that she was not thriving without Christ at the center of her college experience.

I also tutored an amazing young man who once made a comment to me that most average people could never go through in a day what he went through with his disability. I know for Skyler she's felt that most people would be crushed if they had to experience the loneliness she felt inside. Whenever Skyler felt that crushing loneliness, she would open her Bible and read it. It carries her; embracing her relationship with Christ carries her. The faith experience is what carries us. Think about what carries you and your children.

CHAPTER 18

Empowered Living

I t's easy to think that life just happens to us, that we don't really have a say or choice when it comes to how our lives will turn out. I've found that a lot of women around me, whether my sister, friends, or clients, don't feel they even deserve to have a choice in how they live their life. I find particularly that a lot of the Christian women I work with feel guilty doing things for themselves, or even stepping into a place where they have the control to do what they want to do. It's a weird psychology to understand, especially for me, since I believe God gave me free will. I believe that when we are living in our purpose for God, we are living his will. Feeling guilty or undeserving of the right to choose only leads us to live lives where we sit back and wait for things to happen. Thinking we don't have the right to make things happen puts us in the place of living life at the mercy of someone else.

I've experienced living my own life like that. I sat back and waited to make decisions and lived my life waiting for people to tell me what to do. I've lived most of my life letting things happen on other people's time. What I realized was that by living this way, I was putting off living how God really wants me to, just because some person in my world was saying what I could and couldn't do. I was always asking permission from my husband, for example. I am a submissive person, and I wanted my husband to be happy. I was always consulting with him when decisions needed to be made. My husband even told me once that while he appreciated me bringing decisions to him, he also wanted to see me make decisions, that it was okay for me to make decisions. For a lot of the women I come into contact with, they feel stuck because they need someone else to give them the green light or permission to live in their full potential.

It pains me to think of the amount of time I spent in my life staying stuck and not doing things for fear of upsetting someone else. When I set out to write this book, I was signed with a literary agent and was so thrilled that I might find a huge publisher. After a few rejections, however, I felt a bit defeated. I realized, though, that I could either stop or do it anyway. It is no reason not to live to my fullest because I am waiting for someone else to validate what I'm doing.

It was just another opportunity to say yes to myself. This is a big thing, feeling empowered enough to say yes to myself. To know it's okay to start taking chances and not wait for someone else to tell me what I could or couldn't do. It may have taken me a while, but I finally stepped fully out of victim mentality. I could have lived my whole life believing that because I was stuck. We all need to stop being victims and start making decisions and taking chances. I know that investing in myself left me feeling much more empowered.

When we're empowered in our choices and we start making small decisions that are based on what we want and not what someone else wants for us, then we're living an empowered life. For a long time, I wasn't doing that;I wasn't living an empowered life. As a parent of kids with disabilities, I would go into meetings at school with a team of people who were educated and making decisions for my children, yet I was an integral part of that team. When I started to recognize that I have a say as part of the team that influences the direction and choices affecting my child's life, I couldn't sit back and be told how to think. How could I cultivate a strong voice in my child if I myself was not living an empowered life, reaching my own potential and embracing my own inner voice? I made the conscious decision to stop being a person who let things happen to her, and instead became a person who makes things happen for herself.

Once I freed myself from this victim mentality and became empowered, I was able to empower my children. Now I have a daughter who is in college and able to go right into the Dean's office and speak up for herself. Skyler has told me she feels empowered. I don't know that she would feel so empowered if I had not stopped acting like a victim and role modeling living an empowered life. Empowered living is key in watching your children—and your own life—soar.

CHAPTER 19

Living A Life You Love

Raising children in general, and children with disabilities in particular, has required me to dig deep and figure out who I am as an individual. In doing so, what I've found is that I have not always lived. I mean, I'm living life, but am I living a life that I *love?*

As I was raising my kids and we had issues come up with Skyler and Thomas, I would always tell myself at the end of the year that the next year would be different; it would be *my* year to live. Then we would start a new year and have a whole new team of teachers, and I would find myself once again just living life. I was just surviving. I knew there was a big gap between living a life and living a life I loved, and I wanted to bridge that gap.

When I had the epiphany that I was just living my life, I found out about a life purpose coaching training program. I signed up and was connected with an amazing woman named Karen. I chose her because she was a special education teacher. She trained me and walked me through the process of becoming a life coach, which took about a year altogether. Throughout that journey, I had to explore myself. I did a life plan, where I spent two days looking at all the different stages of my life, where I was and what my plan was for the future. Doing this exercise, I realized: if you're not living a life where you're living out your purpose, how can you live a life you love? I knew in that moment that my purpose was to be a life coach.

Prior to this discovery, I thought my purpose was to take this journey and raise my children with disabilities and use my experience to help other moms. I really feel connected to women and their stories, and I feel like an advocate for women. As I worked through my two-day life plan, which was both draining and inspiring, I realized I was not living on purpose, which translated into not living a life that I was passionate about. Although I had loved being a mom, and found the day in and day out process of helping develop valuable individuals rewarding, I knew there was more to life. I also knew I really wasn't modeling what I wanted to my children. By not living a life I loved or was passionate about, I was not modeling the legacy I really wanted to leave. I took a risk when I made the decision to be a life coach. I went to Missouri to stay and train with a woman I had never met. It felt scary to me, and it was the first step I took towards becoming a life coach and, ultimately, living my life with purpose. Being brave enough to knock on a stranger's door was really the start of me developing a life that was deep and fulfilling. A life where I was taking risks and loving all that my life involved.

If we want to live a life that is passionate and purposeful, we have to look hard at ourselves and figure out why we aren't already doing it. As I went through the training with Karen, I had to really put myself out there emotionally. I had to look at my path, review my life in five year increments, and revisit things that had traumatized me. I needed to see what things I had to change. It isn't anyone else's responsibility to help us live a purposeful life we love. Even though we may look to others for support, in the end, it comes down to our willingness to own our choices and take responsibility for our lives. It's not enough anymore to believe that just because we became mothers we can't pursue our dreams. I had to take ownership for where I was, which was living a life of complacency and not taking risks.

The path had been set in motion for me to change even before going to my life coaching training. I decided to train for a marathon, so I trained and finished two marathons. Then, I entered a Mrs. Ohio pageant.

Anyone who knows me knows I love watching the Miss America pageant. I like the glamour of it. When I came across a website for Mrs. Ohio, I decided to enter. Take a risk. Why not? I even hired a pageant coach. I pushed myself so far to do it. It was so much harder than I could have imagined. I was so uncomfortable. I didn't win, and I remember wondering why I took that risk in the first place. I felt like a failure, and it took a while before I really understood that I was a winner the minute I signed up. I was a winner the minute I stepped out of my comfort zone and took a risk. I put myself out there in a way that really stretched me. Would I do it again? Absolutely not! It wasn't for me. But I don't regret it.

The pageant was a step in my journey towards finding the life I love. I started searching for a deeper life experience, and I tried lots of things on the journey. My daughter, Katie, is an excellent athlete, and one day she pointed out to me that she had seen me train and run all these races and marathons, but was I winning the races? I explained that no, I wasn't. But I was trying.

This is something to consider when we reflect on how we live our lives. Are you more worried about winning rather than trying? If you're more worried about winning than taking the risks, you will take a lot longer to get anywhere. I never set out to win the marathon, I chose to run a marathon in order to set goals and prove to myself that I can do things and be okay with not winning. That I can be okay with just engaging in life. How do you live a life you love if you're not willing to take risks and step off the ledge?

It was never about achieving a worldly victory to be judged by all as worthy. It was about finding that victory within myself. Doing something I always wanted to do. Now I'm living a big life for me, and creating a life I'm proud of. I am not sitting back and watching everyone else; I am engaged in life. Being a winner looks different for all of us. I didn't need to win the marathon to participate and feel good about it. I didn't even need to win the pageant to participate and feel good about it. It was still a great experience. It made me confident, and I learned that I didn't need external validation.

Ask what your heart's motivation is for doing this thing, whatever the thing is you want to do. Living a life you ultimately love involves making choices that are really risky. There is no more sitting back and just watching other people living the life you wish you had. I spent a lot of years watching other mothers and wondering how they did it all, and I had to let it go.

I don't wish I had a different life, and I don't want my kids to live a life they wish was different. I want them to live their lives right now. We don't know what life will bring, so living a life you love daily is vital. When I had these feelings about five or six years ago, I felt urgency. I knew I wanted to step out and take chances. I remember being a freshman in college and having a chat with a good friend of mine from the South. She asked me, "Do you want to run with the big dogs or stay on the porch?" Well, it may have taken a few years, but it was time to get off the porch. I want to run with the big dogs. This is what I want my kids to see. I try to live and take chances. My husband is a hunter. He is adventurous and hunts in dangerous places in the world. I knew I didn't want the kids to only see their dad doing these things; I wanted them to see me living adventurously in my own way.

Now, I'm living a life I love by doing things I never thought I'd do. Going back and getting a master's degree in my 40's was a big part of this shift too. I was in a class with a wide range of ages, and the classmates I admire most are the older students, the people in their 50's who decided to come back to school, much like I did. Wow— they are running with the big dogs!

If you think you are sacrificing your happiness and not living your life with purpose and passion, I encourage you to ask yourselves these questions: Is there a difference between just living and living a life you love? What are you modeling to people around you? Your kids? Are you more worried about winning than trying?

I know the answers for me now are completely different to the answers I would have given ten years ago. Check in with yourself. If you answer those questions and you're happy with them, then you're already living a life you love. If you're not happy with the answers, take a look at the life you're living and find out why. The life you love is waiting for you, and it's up to you to dare to step into it.

CHAPTER 20

Embrace A Guide

Even though I have improved my life in many ways, each morning I wake up and I never know if it will be a day where I feel hopeful or a day where I feel hopeless. I now know that it's a daily choice, how I will react to what comes up each day and how I'm going to let it affect what I send out to my children. I have recently felt very stuck, so much so that I just have not been accomplishing any of my goals. It took a call with my business coach to get inspired to finish this book and live out my dream. I just needed a little help from somebody else and the willingness to receive the help.

It is ongoing; it is life. Even when I am on vacation, my daughter might call me crying, struggling. In those moments, sometimes it's easy to wonder if this will ever get better? Will she struggle every day of her life? But I know now that I don't need to stay in those thoughts. In that moment, on that phone call, she is struggling and I can support her. The moment passes. Life goes on.

Watching my children grow up, it seemed so often like Skyler and Thomas were treading water. In truth, it still does. It has been really difficult to navigate the journey. Through so much of it I thought I could do it all on my own, but it was tough. That's really one of the reasons I've felt so passionate about coaching. I felt a call to put myself out there and share my children's story, to let other moms know it's not something we have to do by ourselves. That is often why when I say I cannot tutor one more child, I find time to fit them in because I know how badly moms and these children need help. Often as moms there is a strong message from society that we have to do it all. I think of the Brady Bunch, or those friends I've had who always had a clean home and smiling kids, plus worked full-time. Inherent in this, however, is the idea that it's weak to ask for help. I've spent a long time trying to figure out why I didn't have all the answers, but we'll never have all the answers. We never will. The best thing I did for myself throughout this journey was surrounding myself with people who knew a little more than me, who were willing to share with me along the way.

I have embraced a guide through many different seasons of my life. When I was younger and in my early 30's, it was my own mother. She did not always feel able to advise where Skyler and Thomas were concerned, but she listened to and validated me. We don't necessarily need to surround ourselves with other moms of kids with disabilities, although I did have a period where I resented the mothers of kids who didn't have disabilities. But that resentment just isolated me from the support they were willing to offer. The flipside of this is being around moms of kids who have much more advanced disabilities than yours; sometimes this made me feel guilty. Regardless, in every season of life, the people you come into contact with have a purpose and are there for a reason.

Support comes in many ways; it's important to find what works for you. For some people, support groups like Facebook groups work. For me, they never really worked, as the tendency to take the conversations down the complaining and negative road always seemed to prevail. I have tried different friends and support groups through the years, but the biggest help was finding a life coach. I even found a coach for different areas of my life. I hired a weight-loss coach. I hired a business coach. I hired a life coach. It worked for me because I wasn't struggling to the point where I needed a counselor, but the life coach was highly beneficial. There's a difference between a life coach and a counselor. A life coach takes you where you are and helps move forward with your situation. Life coaching helped me work through the areas in which I felt stuck. Working with a life coach allowed me to step off the ledge and start a new career of coaching and advocacy for women with special needs children. I am now able to give back in a way that I believe is needed.

Although I am blessed to have found some excellent coaches, I never found a coach who actually raised children with special needs to work with. I feel called to coach women because I wish I could have had someone who specifically understood me the same way I now understand other moms of kids with disabilities. I created this business and platform to engage and connect with women. To let them know help is available. This book is a way for me to give tidbits of information, but it's not everything I can help moms with, simply because every mother's situation is different. Reading this book will hopefully touch people who need just a little bit of help getting through raising their children with disabilities or even just being moms and struggling to live a balanced life and have more days that are hopeful than hopeless. Coaching women on a one-on-one level, I get to work with women where they're at. The process is highly individualized because no two women are alike. I hope as I continue to grow, I can make more time to expand my business to offer more one-on-one coaching packages to more clients.

When you are seeking a guide or support, ensure that their testimony lines up with where you want to go. For me, my experience raising my kids, my test, is my testimony. Learn what your options are and who is available for you, and find the person who will help you move forward, help you live a life you love, and help you create your legacy. Coaching is such an intimate relationship; it's worth searching to find the person whose story matches your story. Maybe they're just a little ahead of you, in the direction you want to go. You can also find a course online, and there are many to choose from that are also reasonably priced. We live in a world that makes it possible for us to have the answers and support just a click away. Often, when raising children with disabilities, it's hard to do things and get away from the house, so these online programs or calls are a way of decreasing your isolation and accessing support. I do much of my coaching on the phone or through Skype.

There is absolutely no need to walk this journey alone. You don't know all the answers, and you shouldn't know all the answers. It doesn't take getting a master's degree in special education like I did to find the answers. There are people who are a few steps ahead of you and are able to help you. Coaching for me was an investment that helped me and continues to help me. It has grown my business, connected me with people, and helped me be a better guide for my children. I live a life I feel so much better about.

It is really easy to use money as an excuse to not invest in ourselves, but what we don't realize is that by investing in ourselves, we're investing in becoming better guides for our children. It is that simple: embracing a guide to get help for yourself helps you be a better guide for your children. It's not forever; you're not always going to need that help. When you work with the right people, they won't encourage you to stay stuck. The best guides will move you to a place where eventually you're not going to need them anymore and you're going to be able to navigate this yourself.

A lot has happened in the almost two years since my husband and I dropped Skyler off at college. Skyler made the decision to choose a different university that was more aligned with who she is a learner and overall individual. I remember as she came home at the end of her freshman year on breaks, she just did not seem to be living joyfully. She made comments like, "Well, thank God college is only four years because this is really hard." I remember telling her, "You need to live fully in college; you should not be just surviving, God does not want you to suffer." For some reason, she started listening to everyone around her, but most importantly, she started listening to herself! Now, Skyler is through her second year at a new school and is happier . This is a child that has transformed in so many ways. It is truly inspiring.

Thomas is also so amazing right now. As I write, he is sitting in a tree, having gone deer hunting with his father. This is a young man that is most comfortable in his room watching videos or playing a game. He hates loud noises or gunfire and often reacts by grabbing his ears when he is startled by a sudden noise. He is continuing to challenge himself and has started seeking out relationships with friends or his dad, even if it means he might be uncomfortable. This is so amazing to watch.

The journey and the successes I have mentioned are not because of any one person but a team of people that have blessed both of my children's lives. First of all, their loving sisters, Vivianne and Katie, who often have had to stand in the shadows and not get the attention they needed or wanted at times. The tribe of supporters for each child and my tribe of supporters have made it possible to continue to smile on days that I truly felt hopeless. My husband, Larry, who often had to deal with a distracted and chaotic home when I was just trying to figure things out!

Wherever you are in the path of raising a child with a disability, I understand. I get it. The endless IEP meetings, the lonely days watching your child be left out, the strain on your relationships, the struggle with feeling unhealthy and alone when you have given everything you have to your children. I can tell you it does and will get better, but only if you act boldly and courageously to change your circumstances. Raising a child with a disability is a marathon, but if you want to run at a more comfortable and exhilarating pace, get off the porch and run with the big dogs. Give your children a mother to admire and a legacy that helps them live a life they love. Moving from hopeless to hopeful starts with you.